TARKOVSKY
Cinema as Poetry

also published by Faber

Sculpting in Time
Andrey Tarkovsky

TARKOVSKY
Cinema as Poetry

MAYA TUROVSKAYA

Translated by Natasha Ward
Edited and with an Introduction by Ian Christie

faber and faber
LONDON · BOSTON

First published in 1989
by Faber and Faber Limited
3 Queen Square London WC1N 3AU

Phototypeset by Wilmaset Birkenhead Wirral
Printed in Great Britain by
Richard Clay Ltd Bungay Suffolk

All rights reserved

© Maya Turovskaya, 1989
Translation © Natasha Ward, 1989
Introduction © Ian Christie, 1989

A CIP record for this book is
available from the British Library

ISBN 0–571–14709–7

Contents

List of illustrations vii
Acknowledgements viii

Introduction: Tarkovsky in His Time
    by Ian Christie ix
Note on Russian–English Translation xxvi
From the Author xxviii
Prologue: A World Cleft in Two 1

Part I: Forward to the Past
1 · The Beginning 15
2 · *The Steamroller and the Violin* 22
3 · *Ivan's Childhood* 29
4 · *Andrey Rublyov* 36
5 · *Solaris* 51
6 · *Mirror* 61

Part II
7 · Andrey Tarkovsky's Motifs 75
8 · Space and Time in Tarkovsky's Work 85
9 · Cinema as Poetry 94

Part III: Beyond the Mirror
10 · The Soul's Landscape, After Confession (*Stalker*) 105
11 · From Confession to Sermon (*Nostalgia*) 117
12 · From Sermon to Sacrifice (*The Sacrifice*) 136
Epilogue: After the Retrospective 150

Notes 155
Bibliographical Note 164
Filmography 165
Select Bibliography 170
Index 173

List of illustrations

Frontispiece: Tarkovsky directing *Stalker* (photograph by Grigory Verkhovsky).
1. *Ivan's Childhood*: 'The play of fantasy and imagination'.
2. *Ivan's Childhood*: Ivan going 'over the river' on his last mission.
3. *Ivan's Childhood*: Kolya Burlyaev as Ivan with Lt. Galtsev and Captain Kholin.
4. Kolya Burlyaev as Boriska, the young bell-founder, in *Andrey Rublyov*.
5. *Andrey Rublyov*: the Tartars' savage attack on Vladimir.
6. Anatoly Solonitsyn as Andrey Rublyov, the passive protagonist.
7. *Solaris*: Chris Kelvin aboard the beleaguered space station.
8. *Solaris*: 'the effort of resurrection' as Hari struggles to come alive again.
9. *Mirror*: Margarita Terekhova as the mother – 'proving her immortality'.
10. *Mirror*: personal history recalled through a Breughel composition.
11. Tarkovsky filming Kaidanovsky and Solonitsyn on *Stalker* (photograph courtesy of Evgeny Tsimbal).
12. *Stalker*: the trio of metaphysical adventurers enter the 'Zone'.
13. *Nostalgia*: Gorchakov's 'road to Calvary' across a muddy pool.
14. *Nostalgia*: Domenico calls upon the world to repent, before setting fire to himself on the Capitoline Hill in Rome.
15. *The Sacrifice*: Little Man as a 'seeker' following in his father's footsteps.

Acknowledgements

This book would never have appeared in English without the persistence and resource of Sian Thomas and Renny Bartlett, who first proposed it. The USSR Filmmakers' Association played an important role in facilitating contacts during its preparation and particular thanks are due to Elem Klimov, Inna Kisseleva and Evgeny Tsimbal for practical assistance. Natasha Ward and Walter Donohue displayed patience and generosity far beyond the call of duty during the book's long gestation, as did Patsy Nightingale, when editorial work made impossible demands. Richard Taylor provided valuable advice, as ever. John Roberts of the Great Britain–USSR Society and Adrian Turner, former Guardian Lecture Officer at the National Film Theatre, both made possible Tarkovsky's first visit to Britain and gave me the opportunity to meet him, for which I am in their debt. Bill Pence, Director of Film at the Hopkins Center of Dartmouth College, and Richard Combs, editor of the *Monthly Film Bulletin*, first prompted me to write about Tarkovsky and I am grateful for their encouragement. Stills from Tarkovsky's films are reproduced by courtesy of the Artificial Eye Film Company, Contemporary Films Ltd and BFI Stills, Posters and Designs.

IC

Introduction : Tarkovsky in his Time

In all my ways let me pierce through
Into the very essence,
At work, or following my path,
Or in heartfelt perturbance.

        Boris Pasternak[1]

Make visible what, without you, might never have been seen.

        Robert Bresson[2]

When Andrey Tarkovsky first visited Britain in February 1981 for the launch of *Stalker*, it fell to me to interview him at the National Film Theatre in London on what was, to say the least, a daunting occasion. After years of fruitless invitations, his arrival had been announced with only a few days' notice; yet hundreds of admirers turned out, as they would also in Glasgow and Edinburgh, to see and hear this already legendary figure.

The atmosphere over lunch before the interview was tense. Certainly there were any number of reasons why he might have been wary and uncommunicative, especially with a prominent official from the Soviet cinema ministry, Goskino, in attendance, but nothing prepared me for the transformation that occurred when we went on stage. Now he was candid, uncompromising and passionate. Knowing how easily we could find ourselves adrift on a sea of misunderstanding, given the gulf that separates Soviet and Western attitudes to cinema, I wanted to establish a clear outline of his working situation. Patiently he responded by explaining the advantages of the Soviet production system, which allows directors great freedom and resources to pursue their projects – 'and when we are actually filming, there aren't the same restrictions as elsewhere'.

In conversation he later confirmed the rumour that a large part of *Stalker* had been re-shot with a different cameraman when he eventually saw the rushes and was dissatisfied with them; and several years later I discovered from one of the unit leaders at Mosfilm Studios, the veteran director Yuli Raizman, that the cost of this re-shooting had had to be absorbed by the studio. Now, thanks to Maya Turovskaya's detailed account of the making of *Ivan's Childhood*, we learn that he 'inherited' this quintessentially Tarkovskian project only after another director had failed with it *and* that he was allowed to start completely afresh – an extraordinary and only too rare insight into the actual workings of the Soviet film industry.

The advantage of a state monopoly, Tarkovsky told his London audience, was that 'there is no real connection between size of budget and scale of release', since 'losses on expensive films can be balanced against gains on cheap films'. Did he say this only because his 'minder' was sitting in the front row? I thought not then, and believe even less now that he ever went out of his way to be diplomatic. Indeed, the character that emerges from Turovskaya's study seems, if anything, deliberately provocative. When I asked with studied tact about 'problems' over the release of controversial films, having in mind the notorious four-year delay that *Andrey Rublyov* suffered, his candid, laconic answer spoke volumes:

> To this day I cannot understand why there was such a delay in releasing it. Maybe sometime in the future an historian of the Soviet cinema will discover the true reason. I think many of the problems in this case were due to the fear of those involved with the film's release.[3]

Tarkovsky lived long enough to see – albeit from exile – the fall of his arch-enemy Filip Yermash, the long-serving minister in charge of Goskino, in the wake of the great liberation of Soviet cinema that stemmed from the Film-Makers' Union congress of May 1986. And as directors and critics joined forces to lay bare the shameful secret history of capricious and vengeful censorship that had condemned dozens of films to longer suppression than any of his during the Brezhnev era, he must have felt that his own protest and personal sacrifice had not been in vain.

For there can be little doubt about the impact of the challenge Tarkovsky threw down in 1984, when he publicly demanded assurances from the Soviet authorities concerning his family and his freedom to work if he returned from Italy to Moscow. Along with the international campaign of protest which finally won release from prison for Sergey Paradzhanov, and the less publicized departure for the West of two other leading directors, Andrey Konchalovsky and Otar Ioseliani, Tarkovsky's self-exile dramatized the dilemma facing Soviet cinema on the threshold of a new political regime: to heed the Party's call for more old-fashioned political uplift, and so alienate even more of the most talented film-makers, not to mention the vital youth audience? Or to back the directors, young and old, who were using cinema to attack corruption, complacency and stasis, and others like Tarkovsky, Paradzhanov, Ioseliani, who were challenging the canons of socialist realist prose with new poetic visions?

The struggle was already under way before Brezhnev's death in 1982 – Soviet cinema had never been entirely acquiescent since Stalin's demise – and it continued through the transitional Andropov and Chernenko regimes, which produced a stream of contradictory signals.[4] Then, barely a year after Gorbachev's accession, the Film-Makers' Union took the lead in what soon amounted to a wholesale cultural revolution (students of Soviet history will recall that Stalin's first Five Year Plan was preceded by a great cultural ferment in 1928–9).[5] No sooner had the film-makers thrown out all their compromised officials and proclaimed an end to censorship, than writers and artists in other fields followed suit.

But to portray Andrey Tarkovsky as a 'dissident' would be quite misleading. For he was, undeniably, a product and in many ways a beneficiary of the remarkable institution that Soviet cinema became under Stalin's tutelage, even if he was later to complain bitterly about its treatment of him as an artist. In 1981 he was happy to pay sincere tribute to his teacher, Mikhail Romm, under whom he studied for the statutory six years at the state film school VGIK. Did his praise sound slightly hollow, when he said that Romm 'didn't try to teach us our profession', but 'did everything possible to preserve the individual in each of us' and 'taught us to respect ourselves'? Only if we think of a film school as essentially a place of technical instruction and direction as a set of skills. Tarkovsky was clear that film direction couldn't be taught, one could only 'become' a director by discovering the vocation of an artist.

For the young Tarkovsky and others of his generation who would become a veritable Soviet 'new wave' in the early sixties, grasping the freedom that Khrushchev's 'thaw' had brought, Romm was crucial precisely because he *didn't* teach the tainted socialist realism of the Stalin era. Instead, rather as Renoir did in France for the *nouvelle vague*, he acted as a bridge between two widely separated generations: in this case between the early Soviet avant-garde of the twenties and the first generation to emerge after the war and Stalin's final paranoid years. Romm himself did not start directing until the very end of the Soviet silent era in 1934, but was only three years younger than Eisenstein and later worked with him both at Mosfilm and VGIK. His own films ranged from two of the classic reverential thirties portrayals of Lenin and an early cold war anti-American diatribe to a forward-looking drama of nuclear physicists and a powerful anatomy of the Fascist state (this last co-written by the author of the present book, Maya Turovskaya).[6]

Romm's own career may have been blighted by the dictates of 'the Soviet Union's only important film critic', as Stalin was once ruefully termed. But he outlived Stalin long enough to oversee the difficult transition to a new cinema. Khrushchev's famous 'secret speech' to the Twentieth Party Congress in 1956 had singled out Stalin's obsessive use of cinema to falsify his own record and create an absurdly utopian image of Soviet reality. Now it was up to the new generation of film-makers to liberate their vast audience: but first they had to liberate themselves from two decades of doublethink and rigidly academic technique. It was Romm who pointed the way and, with his own *Nine Days of One Year* in 1962, showed how even an established director could transform his whole way of working. In a way, he managed to pass on the legacy of Eisenstein's 'Socratic' teaching method to a generation robbed, by his early death in 1948, of direct contact with the Soviet cinema's greatest talent.

Many other Soviet directors of Tarkovsky's generation have paid tribute to Romm's remarkable quality of enabling them to discover their own distinctive gift. It was Romm, for instance, who encouraged the self-taught peasant Shukshin to write vernacular stories from his own experience while studying direction at VGIK (coincidentally at the same time as Tarkovsky: the two hated each other, according to a contemporary) which led to Shukshin becoming an acknowledged writer as well as film-maker.

Hence the significance of Turovskaya's opening chapter, which might otherwise be obscure to Western readers. Her first-hand account of Romm introducing that preview screening of *Ivan's Childhood* at the Film-Makers' Union recalls what it actually *felt* like to be part of the first post-thaw generation of young artists and intellectuals. They were determined to break out of the Stalinist straitjacket, revelling above all in the freedom to experiment with style and form which had been so long denied their predecessors. Hence, too, the value of her original article, quoted here, written under the dizzying influence of the film: the claim that *Ivan's Childhood* stakes out a new terrain for 'poetic cinema' was still a bold one amid the fraught cultural politics of the Khrushchev era – soon to end with a new round of 'show trials' presaged by that of Sinyavsky and Daniel, plunging Tarkovsky's generation into what is now referred to as 'the era of stagnation' under Brezhnev.

The years 1959–65 saw a torrent of feature débuts by directors who, apart from what they owed to Romm, had little else in common (Turovskaya also draws attention to a transitional generation, active from 1955, who paved the way for this breakthrough). There was Marlen Khutsiev, with his neo-realist post-war fable *Two Fyodors* (1959) and *cinéma vérité*-influenced *I Am Twenty* (1964); Georgy Danelia with the first of his wry comedies, *Seryozha* (1960); in Georgia, Otar Ioseliani's *April* (1960) was never released and his official début became *When the Leaves Fall* (1967); Larissa Shepitko's *Heat* (1963) was shot in remote Kirghizia, far from Moscow's bureaucrats; her future husband Elem Klimov managed to make his satirical fantasy *Welcome, or No Unauthorised Entry* (1964) while still a student at VGIK, but had to wait until Khrushchev himself approved before timid officials released it; Vasily Shukshin, like Tarkovsky and Klimov, included fantasy sequences in his first feature *There Was a Lad* (1964); Andrey Mikhalkov-Konchalovsky, co-writer of Tarkovsky's graduation short *The Steamroller and the Violin* and of *Andrey Rublyov*, also took the precaution of going to Kirghizia for his own directorial début, *The First Teacher* (1965); and out of Georgia came the exotic, mystical *Shadows of Our Forgotten Ancestors* (1965) by Sergey Paradzhanov.

Soviet cinema was still a state monopoly, but it had stopped being monolithic. Moreover, the isolationism of the Stalin years had been breached, so that the work of Tarkovsky's generation gradually became known abroad, while more (but still not many) foreign films began to reach Soviet audiences and be studied by young Soviet directors. When Tarkovsky was in London in 1981, I was curious to discover what he wanted to see. The answer turned out to be popular genre films, like James Glickenhaus's ultra-violent *The Exterminator*, then enjoying a brief *succès de scandale*. These were what couldn't easily be seen in Moscow and, even if he seemed rather apologetic, it was entirely understandable that any film-maker would want to take the pulse of mainstream (or even down-market) contemporary technique. More prestigious 'art cinema' he already had access to, although current examples like Resnais's *Mon Oncle d'Amerique* seemed of little interest to him ('too mechanical').

He was to make unexpected use of his excursion into pulp movies during our public interview when, doubtless to the surprise of the audience, he declared uncompromisingly that 'there can be no talk of art in relation to films like *The Exterminator*'. This came in the midst of what can be described only as an orthodox Platonic account of the function of art:

> Cinema is a high art . . . It seems to me that the purpose of art is to prepare the human soul for the perception of good. The soul opens up under the influence of an artistic image . . . I could not imagine a work of art that would prompt a person to do something bad . . . My

purpose is to make films that will help people to live, even if they sometimes cause unhappiness – and I don't mean the sort of tears that *Kramer vs Kramer* produces . . . Art can reach to the depths of the human soul and leave man defenceless against good.

Plato, in fact, took a generally dim view of the arts, especially music, poetry and theatre, believing that they were more likely to do harm than good. In the *Republic*, he has Socrates argue that they should be allowed in the ideal state only under strict control, since the passions they arouse are quite unsuited to the development of highly moral character. For Plato there is literally *no* distinction to be made between aesthetics and morality: portrayal of ugliness or evil in art debases the audience, while exposure to beauty and truth produces goodness. And only the good can create a true Republic.

Is this what Tarkovsky really believed? Up to a point, I think it is – and ironically it expresses what was most 'Soviet' about his thinking. For the legacy of Lenin's notorious dictum that 'cinema is for us the most important of all the arts' – still inscribed on the façades of many Soviet cinema buildings – is a profound belief in the power and status of cinema as art. Certainly it is viewed as propaganda too, which was Lenin's immediate concern, but what many in the West fail to understand – until they encounter a Soviet film-maker – is how this tablet of the law has been incorporated into the pantheon of Soviet aesthetics, and how Platonic this pantheon turns out to be. The position which took shape during the early thirties created a kind of contract between artists and the state, based on the assumption that 'good art' would help mould the ideal Soviet Man, who would in turn loyally serve the state. Therefore the state should do everything possible to support the artists, while expecting them wholeheartedly to support it.

Naturally there were disagreements on both sides of the contract – and soon there was Stalin's murderous vendetta against artists, intellectuals and former Bolshevik comrades, which left the survivors cowed and defensive. But what is often forgotten is that the profoundly social and moral theory of art that underpins the whole organization of Soviet culture both predates and postdates Stalin. So in the late fifties, or the late eighties, a critic of the current Soviet regime will often use the same authoritarian and idealistic (in a Platonic sense) terms of argument as his conservative opponent. So too do the most mediocre as well as the best Soviet film-makers, to the chagrin of Westerners who find such ideas quaint, while bemoaning the low status of cinema compared with the traditional fine and performance arts in their own countries.

In other words, the austere aesthetic that Tarkovsky stated in 1981 and continued to preach after his break with the Soviet Union in 1984, is really much closer to a conventional Soviet outlook than might be supposed – even though he clearly despised the bulk of Soviet film production, together with those responsible for supervising, censoring and interpreting it. For some, perhaps a majority, of his Western admirers this insistence on the absoluteness and autonomy of art may be a welcome antidote to the prevailing attitudes they know only too well. It confirms their reaction against the overt politicization of cinema (most Soviet cinema is studiously non-political), against experimentation, against the journalistic and naturalistic influence of television.[7] It restores art, understood in a purist sense, to its proper centrality.

But for others – and here I must include myself – it is a position that leaves too many questions unanswered, however much one respects Tarkovsky's actual films. From where we stand now, it involves turning the clock back (or forward) to some utopian ideal, and denying what have undeniably been powerful social, political and technological influences on the most complex art form yet developed. To continue basing our aesthetics on ethics since the onset of modernism is also to deny the epistemological, semiotic and indeed ludic aspects of art. The demand that it should astonish us isn't merely flippant – we recognize that reality is multiple and contradictory, so art can make us see and experience differently, hypothetically. Nor does Tarkovsky's distinction between high and low art seem very clear cut, especially when he aligns it with the equally dubious choice between non-commercial and commercial art. It was no less than Erwin Panofsky, dean of Renaissance iconographic studies, who wrote in his essay 'Style and Medium in the Motion Picture':

While it is true that commercial art is always in danger of ending up as a prostitute, it is equally true that noncommercial art is always in danger of ending up as an old maid. Noncommercial art has given us Seurat's *La Grande Jatte* and Shakespeare's sonnets, but also much that is esoteric to the point of incommunicability. Conversely, commercial art has given us much that is vulgar or snobbish (two aspects of the same thing) to the point of loathsomeness, but also Dürer's prints and Shakespeare's plays.[8]

When Tarkovsky observed during our discussion that 'cinema is the only art that has its origins in the bazaar', he clearly felt that this was a stigma to be overcome by the production of more masterpieces to 'prove that it is capable of higher things'. But according to Panofsky, expressing what has become almost a commonplace, 'the movies have re-established that dynamic contact between art production and art consumption which ... is sorely attenuated, if not entirely interrupted, in many other fields of artistic endeavour'. In point of fact, almost all the film-makers that Tarkovsky most admired – Ford, Mizoguchi, Fellini – worked in a thoroughly commercial context, and often in relatively despised genres. Only a Soviet director, freed of all commercial responsibility by the state, could be so dismissive of commercially viable endeavour.

No doubt it was also his experience working in Soviet cinema that fuelled Tarkovsky's intense hostility to any *interpretation* of his films, at least in the sense of revealing a hidden meaning. Officially sponsored critiques of works of art have an altogether more sinister significance in the Soviet context than our journalistic tradition comprehends. At any rate, Turovskaya notes that even her article in praise of *Ivan's Childhood* led to 'long, unresolved arguments' with him. Later she provides crucial evidence that helps us to understand at least one source of Tarkovsky's suspicion. The analysis of a passage from Yutkevich's *Skanderbeg* quoted from Tarkovsky's film-school essay shows precisely how a new generation started to question what was taken for granted by their predecessors.[9] Yutkevich belonged to the same generation as Eisenstein and Romm and had thus served his apprenticeship in the 'montage' tradition, learning to make visual metaphors. But a technique which was fresh and powerful in silent films like Eisenstein's *Battleship Potemkin* and *October* soon became academic in the mainly narrative cinema of the sound era. And when used for deliberate 'folkloric' effect in 1954, it must have seemed positively archaic. While seeming to offer the audience something 'artistic', the intercut shot of a breaking wave actually both distracts and insults their intelligence.

Henceforth Tarkovsky would steadfastly reject all metaphor and deny any allegorical intention in his own films. Partly he was reacting against the decadence of the montage tradition – and his identification of this with Eisenstein led him to repudiate Eisenstein too, although little of his later writing and teaching was known during Tarkovsky's formative years. Like the post-war German artists who faced the task of 'de-Nazifying' and renewing their language, whatever medium they worked in, so Tarkovsky's post-Stalin generation felt the imperative to 'make it new'. This meant not only finding new forms in place of the Stalinist genres – the patriotic epic, the exemplary biography, the hymn to self-sacrifice, the struggle to unmask saboteurs – but also getting audiences to *see* things 'in their own right', not as symbols.

Tarkovsky's first films, *The Steamroller and the Violin* and *Ivan's Childhood*, both show this process of renewal at work. As Turovskaya describes it, without any excess of hindsight, the first is clearly trying to strip away sentiment and enable the spectator to see the physical setting and the characters afresh; while the second is a remarkably radical distortion of the well-established Soviet war story genre. Not only is it framed and punctuated by vivid dreams, so that we see the war from Ivan's traumatized viewpoint, but the episodes of Kholin and Masha in the forest, and Ivan playing at war in the church crypt that serves as a field station, take Soviet cinema into new areas of emotional ambiguity and spirituality. It is worth noting, however, that others were also moving in such directions: even the stalwart Raizman set a crucial scene between the tragic teenage couple of *Can This Be Love?* (1961) in a church.

In sequences like these, Tarkovsky doesn't want us to jump to conclusions: he wants us to attend first to the rhythm and framing of images, to experience the film on an aesthetic-intuitive level before considering it intellectually. In his book *Sculpting in Time* he includes a telling anecdote from the making of *Andrey Rublyov*.[10] The original script called for a peasant to launch himself from the cathedral tower on a pair of home-made wings, before crashing to his death. But something seemed wrong with this – too symbolic of human aspiration in the abstract; too closely linked with the myth of Icarus (shades of the breaking wave!)? The solution was to make the peasant's flying machine a primitive balloon, patched together from skins and rags, which dispels the 'spurious rhetoric' of the scene and transforms it into 'a concrete happening, a human catastrophe'. The method recalls Auden's account of the everyday context in which the Old Masters portrayed suffering:

> They never forgot
> That even the dreadful martyrdom must run its course
> Anyhow in a corner, some untidy spot . . .
> Where the dogs go on with their doggy life[11]

And indeed it is the 'untidy spots' where 'dreadful martyrdom' attracts no great sympathy or attention that Tarkovsky made his own terrain in the post-industrial and post-classical landscapes of *Stalker* and *Nostalgia*.

But a considerable amount of *Sculpting in Time* is devoted to attacking the very idea of interpretation, and condemning the influence of Eisenstein, whom Tarkovsky considered the architect of 'intellectualist' cinema. How seriously can we take this polemic?

The point has already been made that, as a VGIK student in the late fifties, what Tarkovsky encountered would have been more a parody of Eisensteinian montage theory than the real thing. Eisenstein's reputation had been in eclipse since before his death in 1948 and the bulk of his writings began to be published only in 1961. At this period, a selective account of Eisenstein's early teaching was routinely attacked as 'formalist', while he was dismissed as a mere theorist rather than an artist.[12] Something of this officially encouraged denigration, ironically, appears in Tarkovsky. Yet a contemporary of his at VGIK recalls his immense enthusiasm for the second part of Eisenstein's *Ivan the Terrible*, which had been 'shelved' for nearly fifteen years and was released only in 1957.[13] This excitement, too, is indeed faithfully recorded in *Sculpting in Time* – although Tarkovsky's 'theoretical' objection to Eisenstein's thoroughgoing composition of all aspects of the film obliges him to question whether it is, properly, 'a cinematic work'![14] Moreover, it seems quite possible that the seeds of Tarkovsky's own great historical fresco *Andrey Rublyov* came from his response to Eisenstein's time bomb. After all, the historical world of the mysterious Rublyov, not to mention his biography, had to be entirely 'composed' before they could be subjected to Tarkovsky's 'principle of direct observation'.

But even if Tarkovsky was perhaps more influenced by prevailing attitudes among the Soviet intelligentsia than he realized, his intuition was not necessarily wrong.[15] And it seems to me that many of his most ardent supporters and denigrators alike have failed to realize the profound importance of the aesthetic he outlined in *Sculpting in Time*.

The core of this is simple, and there is no need to accept all the metaphysical baggage that goes with it in Tarkovsky's essentially symbolist outlook. He begins by noting that what the film camera records is *time*: the time of shooting and its temporal content are, as it were, inscribed in the shot. And so when the director sets about constructing his film from a mass of filmed material, he is literally working with time.[16]

Now this view comes very close to a celebrated account of the 'ontology of the photographic image' in an essay by the French critic and father of the New Wave, André Bazin:

> ... photography does not create eternity, as art does, it embalms time rescuing it simply from its own corruption.
>
> Viewed from this perspective, the cinema is objectivity in time. Film is no longer content to preserve the object ... as the bodies of insects are preserved intact, out of the distant past, in amber ... Now, for the first time, the image of things is likewise the image of their duration, change mummified as it were.[17]

Again, it scarcely matters whether Tarkovsky found this formulation in Bazin or not: what matters is how he develops the idea of a 'double articulation' (my term, not his) of time in cinema. There is, he notes, the time already inscribed in individual shots and there is the necessary, but fraught, *manipulation* of this time by the director as he compiles these diverse time-fragments into a new temporal construct which is the film the spectator will experience. Speaking as a film-maker, Tarkovsky observes that the director cannot force his material into a preconceived structure: he must learn to discern the temporal rhythm already present and work *with* rather than against this.

The persuasive analogy he uses is that of the sculptor, who must respect the nature of his given, or rather chosen, physical material. And this in turn evokes Michelangelo's neo-platonic conception of sculpture as the revelation or discovery of a form that, at least potentially, *already exists* within the marble: 'The greatest artist has no conception which a single block of marble does not potentially contain within its mass, but only a hand obedient to the mind can penetrate to this image.'[18] Compare this with Tarkovsky:

> What is the essence of a director's work? We could define it as sculpting in time. Just as a sculptor takes a lump of marble, and inwardly conscious of the features of his finished piece, removes everything that is not part of it – so the film-maker, from a 'lump of time' made up of an enormous, solid cluster of living facts, cuts off and discards whatever he does not need.[19]

A number of consequences follow from this central insight. First, Tarkovsky conceives of the audience as going to the cinema 'for time: for time lost or spent or not yet had' – which indeed valuably draws attention to the way that any film dilates and compresses the audience's perception of time, just as much as it 'moves' them in an imaginary space. But it may also have led him down the dangerous path of 'aestheticizing' time by unduly protracting it in the last films. Conscious that the shot has a 'time pressure' of its own, Tarkovsky tended to elaborate ever longer shots containing a multiplicity of time traces. The long candle ritual in *Nostalgia* and the final tableau shot in *The Sacrifice* are cases in point, where, especially in the latter, narrative and logistical manipulation (the audience has plenty of time to consider both) may have defused any 'real' time experience. But in *Ivan's Childhood*, *Andrey Rublyov* and *Mirror* he succeeded in creating compelling new rhythms by controlling the 'flow' of time from shot to shot and through whole sequences.[20]

Tarkovsky was not primarily a teacher or a philosopher; if he found himself increasingly cast in the role of a prophet, it was because of the intensity of response that his films evoked. But he steadfastly refused to be drawn into a critical exposition or dialogue about them. Instead he would recall the Zen master who struck his pupil rather than explain (i.e. forced the pupil to discover for himself), or urge his viewers, in Christian style, to become like children:

> We have forgotten how to relate emotionally to art: we treat it like editors, searching in it for that which the artist has supposedly hidden. It is actually much simpler than that, otherwise art would have no meaning. You have to be like a child – incidentally children understand my pictures very well and I haven't met a single serious critic yet who could stand knee-high to those children.

Nor was the problem of audiences hungry for interpretation confined to the West, Tarkovsky admitted: 'In Moscow I often meet viewers and I usually fight with them and try to make them like children, generally without success.' He then outlined a new project on which he was working that, it seemed to me, was as much an account of his own situation as an approach to Dostoevsky's *The Idiot*:

> Many things have been ascribed to Dostoevsky which just aren't true. For example, people everywhere – including Moscow – think of him as a religious writer. But it does not seem to have occurred to them that he was not so much religious as one of the first to express the drama of the man in whom the organ of belief has atrophied. He dealt with the tragedy of the loss of spirituality. All his heroes are people who would *like* to believe but cannot . . . He managed never to talk about this directly, but all his life he suffered because he was unable to believe . . . That is the point of view I want to take in treating Prince Myshkin.

This was already an established theme in his occasional writings and public statements in the Soviet Union; and it would become familiar from the interviews and speeches of his last years, spent mainly in the West. Indeed it could be taken as the basis of his whole aesthetic, which aims at a direct, unmediated communication with the willing spectator. How much this passionate rejection of critical or theoretical 'interference' was a reaction against the explicitly ideological role played by published criticism in the Soviet Union, we can only guess. But it clearly meant that no critic, however sympathetic, could expect much respect from Tarkovsky – as the author of this book discovered.

The result of this hostility towards analysis has been, I think, unfortunate. It has encouraged a rather solemn 'Tarkovskian' style of response to Tarkovsky's films among those who share his suspicion of the intellect in relation to art. And it has almost certainly repelled many who would find much of aesthetic value and intellectual interest in both his films and the (sometimes clumsy) writings. Like that other great radical and seeming mystic, Bresson, Tarkovsky needs rescuing from at least his most imitative admirers.

He also needs to be (re)placed in the Russian and Soviet context which produced him as an artist and, whatever the slings and arrows of bureaucracy, gave him a vast and appreciative audience throughout much of his truncated career. What makes the appearance of Maya Turovskaya's account of Tarkovsky's career and her sympathetic reading of the films so important is that she belongs to the same generation as Tarkovsky and was, like him, a protégé of Mikhail Romm's. Apart from clarifying some important matters of fact, she draws upon a range of references – to poets as often as to critics or other film-makers – that is obviously closer to Tarkovsky's world than the well-meaning, but often unidiomatic, efforts of some Western admirers to penetrate his opaqueness.

Equally important, perhaps, is that Turovskaya's admiration for his work does not blind her to a strain of arrogance and self-mythology in his character. Reading the copious press coverage on his exile, one finds repeated claims that his films were denied screenings in the Soviet Union, while other information suggests virtually the opposite – that for films of obvious minority appeal they reached extraordinarily large audiences.[21] But reliable statistics on Soviet cinema are notoriously hard to find. So to discover the truth about allegations that his films were kept out of Moscow cinemas, Turovskaya tabulated every issue of *Kino nedelya*, the weekly listings paper, for 1972–8 and concluded that at least one, sometimes two or three, of his films were showing for 87.5 per cent of this period. This confirms my own impression that his films were in fact widely available; and the often-quoted complaint that they were relegated to obscure or third-rate cinemas seems based on unfamiliarity with the cumbersome Soviet cinema system, which has few repertory houses and little scope to re-run older films, since the limited number of copies rarely survive even a first release.

Does this detail matter? I believe it does when sweeping statements about Tarkovsky's mistreatment were used to bolster his 'martyr' status in the West. There can be no doubt that he was disliked and at times badly used by the Goskino bureaucracy, but equally he was granted privileges that most Western film-makers could only dream of, and he was secure in the knowledge that he had a huge, devoted audience among the ordinary Russian viewers that he claimed he valued most.

It is equally certain that Maya Turovskaya's book, first published in a West German edition as *Andrei Tarkovsky: Film als Poesie, Poesie als Film* in 1981, could never have appeared in the Soviet Union at this time. Even to write it 'for export' must have required considerable courage. But Turovskaya has long been recognized as a critic and historian of integrity, writing about theatre as well as cinema, and it is fitting that hers should be what is almost certainly the first book by a leading Soviet film critic to be translated into English and published abroad. The original text was substantially revised in 1986–7 to take account of Tarkovsky's last three films and his death in 1986. And in the new climate that resulted from the Film-Makers' Union declaring war on bureaucracy and censorship in May 1986, it is now due to be published soon for the first time in the Soviet Union, with additional material that Maya Turovskaya has gathered during the period of *glasnost*.

When it does appear, the response will no doubt be overwhelming. For Tarkovsky has undergone virtual canonization in the Soviet Union since his untimely death in exile. His films are widely and regularly shown and he is openly spoken of as the greatest modern Soviet film-maker – I still remember the shock of hearing a Goskino official confide that, with his death, Soviet cinema had lost its only figure of international standing. Already there is an informal 'Tarkovsky school' of young film-makers in Leningrad who readily acknowledge his inspiration on their work. One of these is Konstantin Lopushansky, who served his student apprenticeship on the production of *Stalker*, and whose diploma short *Solo* (1983) and feature *Letters from a Dead Man* (1986) betray an obvious (perhaps too obvious) stylistic debt. Another is Aleksandr Kaidanovsky who, as an actor, played the eponymous hero of *Stalker*. Encouraged and later taught by Tarkovsky at the Higher Directors' Courses in Moscow, Kaidanovsky has directed two shorts (one based on a Borges story) and a highly regarded first feature, *An Ordinary Death* (1987), adapted from Tolstoy's *The Death of Ivan Illich*. Perhaps the leading 'Tarkovskian', however, is Aleksandr Sokurov. He had worked at Lenfilm Studios in Leningrad for a decade before the Film-Makers' Union Conflict Committee established in mid-1986 brought his, along with many others', work out of limbo and into circulation.

Sokurov is known to have been Tarkovsky's main hope for the future of personal artistic film-making in the Soviet Union; and so he was commissioned by the Union to make a film specially for the memorial ceremony held at Dom Kino in Moscow in April 1987 on the anniversary of his birth. *Moscow Elegy* has yet to be seen in the West, but Sokurov believes that Tarkovsky's uncompromising artistic principles and personal example count for more than his style. And these, he believes, may be vital to Soviet cinema as it undergoes the upheaval of *perestroika*.

From an outsider's standpoint, it seems clear that Sokurov is right and we must hope that his view prevails. At a memorial service for Tarkovsky held at St James's Church in London (where Tarkovsky had spoken on his last visit to Britain) in January 1987, I was asked to speak on behalf of the British Film Institute. I remembered a passage from Clarence Brown's great book on the Russian poet Mandelstam, which was a memorial address marking the death of the composer Skriabin in 1915, and I quoted from it:

> Pushkin and Skriabin are two transformations of one sun . . . Twice the death of an artist has gathered together the Russian people and lighted a sun above them. Both Pushkin and Skriabin furnished an example of *soborny* Russian death, they died a full death, as some live full lives. In dying, their personality expanded to the dimensions of a symbol of the entire nation.[22]

Mandelstam, who himself perished in Stalin's terror, went on to claim that 'the death of an artist should not be excluded from the chain of his creative achievements, but should be looked upon as the last closing link'. If there is any consolation to be had from Tarkovsky's untimely death, it is surely that the momentum of change in his native Russia has made it possible for him to be publicly mourned and for his example to be freely available to younger generations, to accept or reject.

Ian Christie
London, 1988

Note on Russian–English translation

This translation of Russian into English raises many problems. Probably the least important, but the most irritating, is that of transliteration from the Cyrillic into the Roman alphabet. None of the existing systems is altogether satisfactory; different systems are used in different Romance-language countries (as the Bibliography demonstrates) and rarely are the systems applied with absolute consistency. Tradition, for instance, obliges us to retain the anachronistic 'Tchaikovsky', (German: 'Tschaikowsky') rather than adopt the phonetic 'Chaikovski', although from the same period we have 'Chekhov', instead of 'Tchekhov' (as in French); and there is an understandable urge to familiarize 'Filipp' into 'Philip', 'Aleksandr' into 'Alexander' and the like. Although the current trend among Anglo-Saxon Slavists is to use 'i' rather than 'y' for the Russian 'и', 'Andrey Tarkovsky' is used throughout this book rather than 'Andrei Tarkovski' (or the scholarly 'Tarkovskii') in deference to the original edition of *Sculpting in Time* and other well-known Russian names mostly follow suit, while newly translated names observe more contemporary practice with, for instance, 'zh' rather than 'j'.

A more serious dilemma of transliteration for non-specialist readers is how to convey pronunciation without sacrificing accuracy. Thus to write 'Rublev' for Рублев does not reveal that this name and film title is actually pronounced 'Rublyov' – the Russian 'e' being mostly pronounced 'ye' and sometimes 'yo' ('Potemkin' would be more helpfully rendered as 'Potyomkin'). In general I have tried to convey pronunciation through transliteration wherever possible.

Finally, there is the vexed matter of how to deal with Russian's lack of the definite or indefinite article. Taking this at face value has given us, in cinema history, such staccato titles as *Strike*, *Mother* and *Mirror*, which surely should be *The Strike*, *The Mother* and *The Mirror* (or perhaps *A Mirror*). We do not usually refer to Dostoevsky's novel as *Idiot*; and its's worth reflecting that if Tarkovsky's last film had been made in the USSR, it would probably have reached us as *Sacrifice*. I have introduced such articles as seem valid in English usage.

IC

From the Author

This book was written in bursts, straight from the heart. It was started after the first showing of *Ivan's Childhood*, and built up gradually as a series of reviews, some of which found a publisher, some of which did not. In 1976, after *Mirror*, I put them together and added some extra material – which I suppose I could now call 'archive material' – along with three analytical chapters, 'Andrey Tarkovsky's Motifs', 'Space and Time in Tarkovsky's Work', and 'Cinema as Poetry'.

In fact, there was no such thing as a 'Tarkovsky archive'. There were earlier versions of the screenplays tucked away in the cupboards of the Mosfilm editorial offices, and there was a file on each of the films. There was also a tape of his lectures that Tarkovsky had given me, and his own writings, but I tried to refer as little to these as I did to the interviews – which at the time, of course, were just ordinary conversations – since I did not want my book simply to be a re-hash of Tarkovsky's own articulated aims and intentions as a film-maker.

In 1981 the book was published, not at home, but in West Germany, in an edition where I was aided immeasurably by the fact that Tarkovsky asked his constant collaborator, M. Chugunova, to help me in any way she could.

Now that Andrey Tarkovsky is dead, his 'second life' is gathering momentum with the publication of a plethora of new material – both his own and other people's. If I were starting to write now, the book would probably be completely different. But the book remains what it was from the very beginning: the spontaneous reactions of one cinema-goer, whose only claim can be that she viewed these films with her eyes and ears and heart wide open. In that sense it stands as a witness to its time.

Frontispiece: Tarkovsky directing *Stalker* (photograph by Grigory Verkhovsky).

Prologue : A World Cleft in Two

In the early spring of 1962 the 'language of film' was once again under discussion at the Film-Makers' Union: the whole Soviet cinema was in a ferment of self-questioning and these discussions were the very air it breathed. I remember Mikhail Romm at the close of one of our meetings, saying with great emotion something like: 'My friends, the film we are going to see today is something extraordinary. Something the like of which has never been seen on our screens before. Believe me, it is the work of a very great talent. The director's name is Andrey Tarkovsky.'

Two hours later we emerged from the small viewing theatre baffled and curious, not knowing whether to criticize the author of the film for our confusion or whether to set aside our usual criteria and surrender ourselves to the strange world that had flickered for a short while on the screen before us.

The film was *Ivan's Childhood*. People reacted in different ways, but one thing was sure: an important new director had emerged. Now, of course, some things in the film appear ingenuous and dated, but its magic remains potent to this day.

Under the influence of my vivid first impressions, I wrote a long article on the film for the *Literary Gazette*.[1] It was the first long article to be written about Tarkovsky, and what follows is the original text, which was only published in part at that time:

A World Cleft in Two

The young director Andrey Tarkovsky's film *Ivan's Childhood* is based on Vladimir Bogomolov's novella *Ivan*.[2] In the story, the narrator is a young lieutenant who recounts a series of chance meetings with Ivan, a twelve-year-old reconnaissance agent whose whole family has been killed. The main character is shown 'from outside', in the firm documentary style that distinguished the prose of so many of our young war writers. You could easily imagine the story being transferred to the screen just as it is. It would be an excellent film . . . but a 'prose' film, and very different from the film which Tarkovsky actually made.

Tarkovsky filmed from a diametrically opposite point of view, showing us not Ivan at war, as seen through the eyes of the lieutenant, but the lieutenant, the war and everything else as seen through the eyes of Ivan.

This question of 'point of view' is, of course, by no means an irrelevant one. The important thing is that after so many war films, one should be produced in 1962 by a director from Ivan's own generation, and that it should be so different from the tradition of war films from which it springs.

Bogomolov's story started with the arrival at battalion HQ of a young stranger, soaking and frozen stiff. The film, however, begins very differently, in a calm idyllic setting bathed in summer sunlight: far off a cuckoo is calling, while a butterfly hovers about a tow-headed boy; the huge liquid eyes of a little goat glisten, while the boy's mother smiles her gentle, maternal smile . . . These are images of childhood and silence, with no mention of 21 June 1941[3] or of geographical location. We are gradually led from disconnected, but easily recognizable, images of light, peace and happiness . . . to the war . . .

War enters the film not in its usual trappings: not through a radio announcement, not with the noise of bombers and the streak of anti-aircraft shells, not with the death and destruction that were to invade everyday life and become everyday things in themselves. Not, in fact, as war has been depicted in so many Soviet films before *Ivan's*

Childhood. War enters this film as the heart's remembering, as a sudden and painful jolt to the imagination, when the mother's face is suddenly flung upside-down . . .

The inverted image is a metaphor, the significance of which goes much deeper than its first, obvious meaning. It is also an emotional blow, a sudden loss, a catastrophe, and the whole montage-structure of the film proceeds through a series of such catastrophes. This moment also marks the transition from dream to reality.

Reality is the threatening darkness of a shed from which Ivan must creep out unnoticed. Outside lies the empty, trampled earth. The skeleton of a windmill raises its bony arms to heaven, and over the abandoned fields stands a sinister symptom of war, a burnt-out combine harvester, black and terrible in the conflagration of the sunset.

This conflagration of the sunset is also a metaphor – one which stands firmly in a cultural tradition that includes Urusevsky's 'evil sun', Sholokhov's 'black sun' and the eclipse which 'barred the way' to the troops in *The Lay of Igor's Campaign*, as well as Blok's

> Above the ice, that sphere is harsh and red
> As anger, vengeance, and as blood!

These resonances amplify and extend the metaphor.[4]

The film exists in its own merciless climate, where the landscape is an image of war and of an irreparable jolt to the imagination. The forest is dead, indifferent, awash in floodwater. Ivan is now no longer the tow-headed boy, running carefree after a butterfly, but a scout stealing across his own mother-earth, through the black tree-trunks and the sad marshes; a wolf-cub, suspicious and a loner even among his own kind.

When the wet and shivering little creature first appears at the battalion's field station with the peremptory demand that they telephone 'No. 51' (a higher rank than they are allowed to contact directly) First Lieutenant Galtsev suddenly looks like a foolish boy beside Ivan, although in Soviet war films it is usually the first lieutenant who represents worldly wise maturity. None of the sweet charm of childhood lingers in the face of Ivan – dark as though it had been scorched; or in the guarded scowl and unpleasant bossiness in his voice that reveal his full awareness of his own considerable military importance. This is a grown-up face, experienced and hardened.

The battalion's field station, too, differs in the film from that of the story, in that it becomes not merely the scene of the action, but an image and a symbol. In the original story, Bogomolov uses various visual details and familiar military terms to create the everyday reality of a wartime field station. These details are faithfully reproduced in the film: the paraffin lamp made of old cartridge-cases, the glass which serves as an inkwell. But in the film, every detail also serves to undermine this everyday quality, whether in the uneven light of that very convincing lamp, as it picks out in the darkness, first, an apparently lifeless sleeping arm, then some words scratched on the wall, then part of the vaulting; or indeed the very fact that the field station is located in the crypt of an abandoned church. For Tarkovsky, the choice of a ruined church, with a bell still in one piece where it fell on the floor, is no mere whim. Nor should it be interpreted as part of the fashionable Russian religious revival. The words of farewell scratched on the wall of the crypt – 'There are eight of us, none over nineteen. They're taking us out to kill us. Avenge our deaths!' – make clear the larger meaning of this symbolic conjunction: it brings into the film the important themes of history and historical continuity.

Images crying out for vengeance cling to Ivan throughout.

The film-maker clearly establishes the aesthetic parameters of his imagery when he fills the screen with Dürer's sinister Horsemen of the Apocalypse, the crowds crushed in terror beneath the horses' hooves. This icon of total violence is introduced by a perfectly realistic and acceptable turn of the plot: Ivan is turning the pages of a picture-book captured from a German. The curiosity with which he closely examines it is coloured by hatred. Besides the image itself, we are shown its subjective, 'psychological' refraction through the mind of Ivan. The artificiality of the medium chosen for his work by the great German artist passes unnoticed by the boy. He takes this harrowing, distorted image of violence and suffering as a realistic depiction of the world around him.

A WORLD CLEFT IN TWO

The end of the film contains a montage of German newsreels, including the charred and twisted corpse of Goebbels and the thin little corpses of his children whom he had killed. In other hands, this familiar device might be merely ironic, but here the documentary sequences have a symbolic resonance and complexity as the culmination of the many symbols present elsewhere in the film. It focuses the theme of vengeance, reinforced, as if by assonance, by the empty SS greatcoat hanging on the wall (at the field station an empty greatcoat had, momentarily, personified for Ivan the concept of 'the enemy'). It also intensifies the related theme of a childhood twisted and destroyed. And, of course, its most obvious meaning is the end, the suicide, of Fascism.

The newsreels are also important to the film's aesthetics. Between these two irruptions of an alien, German world and an alien style – between the harsh artificiality of Dürer and the harsh reality of the newsreels – comes the depiction of the war itself: ruined, flooded roads straggling with troops; two lonely figures wandering across an empty field, a captured 'Fritz' and his guard; deformed trees and twisted metal; the skeleton of a crashed plane, still bearing its swastika, sticking out of 'our' bank like a strange tree nurtured by the war; on 'their' bank the corpses of two Soviet scouts swing from a gibbet bearing a placard: 'Welcome'.

This war film depicts no tangible enemies: any depiction, realistic or symbolic, would ring equally false. The 'German' theme enters the film only as a kind of counterpoint, a contrast between image and sound. On the screen we see Ivan compiling his report from the *aides-mémoire* he carries in his pocket: so many grains of wheat, so many pine-cones, so many ears of barley standing for enemy battalions and divisions. On the soundtrack we hear marching boots and German speech, as though he were again re-living the memory. Indistinct German commands, snatches of incomprehensible conversation, surge into Ivan's memory, awake and asleep; it is an alien, unknown language echoing in a land that should be his. This is the litany of invasion, intervention and violence that Russia has known ever since the time of the Tartars. The image of his mother's killing merges with the image of the executed hostages when the little scout, left alone at the field station, 'plays at war'. His game is one played to the final victory, but it is a victory that can never repay all the losses that he has suffered. He hauls the bell on to a beam and beats the alarm. The small bell is shot from a low angle so as to appear enormous. Its alarm will ring out throughout the whole world.

The generation to which both Tarkovsky and the hero of his film belong was hit by the war in a different way from that of their fathers and elder brothers. Those who were older reacted rationally, conscious that in going to war they were fulfilling their duty. The corresponding reaction in the heart of Ivan is an emotional dislocation, and it is this which creates a subtle barrier between Ivan and the adults fighting the war – not only young Lieutenant Galtsev, but also his courageous fellow scout Captain Kholin, his wise old friend Katasonych and the fatherly Lieutenant-Colonel Gryaznov. For them, fighting the war is not only a duty, it is also a job at which they work honestly and selflessly, risking their lives if need be. But for Ivan there can be no such thing as 'time on' and 'time off', no rest and recuperation, no ranks or rewards for services; nothing, in fact, but the reality of the war itself. His need to be in the thick of the war is absolute, stronger than any hierarchy of ranks. He can even grab 'No. 51' by the lapels and shake him when he orders Ivan sent back to enrol in the junior military academy. Strong as his feelings are for Kholin, Katasonych and Gryaznov, he is ready to leave them at once and trudge off down the muddy roads of war as soon as the threat to send him back behind the Soviet lines grows too real. 'I've no one left,' he tells Gryaznov, 'I'm all alone.' Alone with the war. That is why there is no trace of any attempt to depict the mundane realities of the last war, or of the peace which followed.

Images of war and violence are the only absolute reality for Ivan. Sleep and dreams are the only respite that he is granted. Ivan's dreams are not 'memories' in the exact sense of the word, but images of freedom, the play of fantasy and imagination, vaguely pantheistic images of *natural* living, peace and joy . . .

Apples beneath the rain. A dark-haired girl riding in the back of a lorry, and a tow-headed boy offering her an apple. Trees strangely white, as though in negative, rushing past with the road, while dreamy horses nibble unhurriedly at the apples scattered over the unmarked sand, clear and damp from the rain . . .

The world is cleft in two, and there is no place of transition, no interface between the two. Everyday life and everyday details could have been that interface, showing how man can adapt to the hostile climate of wartime. In the story, for Galtsev, it is indeed so. But in the film, for Ivan, these do not exist. Instead, there is a gulf between the two halves of the world, in one of which he exists as a free, complete person, in harmony with the beauty of the world and human feelings, while in the other he is nothing more than a tool for vengeance, ready to destroy his very self for the sake of his mission. This is a reality not only for Ivan. It is the unifying idea of the film's author and as such it is experienced to some degree by all the characters.

There is also another theme, linked to the main trajectory of Ivan's story by association rather than by plot.

Masha, a lieutenant in the medical corps, was formerly a schoolgirl from the countryside outside Moscow. She bears a strange resemblance to the dark-haired little girl in Ivan's dreams, and is as much out of place in the harsh reality of war as those dreams, as childhood itself, as the grove of white-trunked birch trees still miraculously standing – in spite of the loss of some of them for lining trenches. Masha is an island of beauty, like the folk-song on the old Chaliapin record 'Masha must not cross the river', which we never hear to the end.

It is not prudishness or hypocrisy that makes Kholin send Masha away, after courting her in the birch grove. In war, as it is shown in this film, love is an impossibility. The harrowing longing in the relationship between Kholin and Masha, like Ivan's deep longing for happiness, is a symptom of a life that has careered off its appointed course.

The river has 'our' bank, and 'theirs': on 'our bank', the skeleton of the German plane with the swastika; on 'theirs', the two corpses with the placard saying 'Welcome' in Russian. The job of Kholin and Galtsev is to get Ivan over to the other side, where once again he will take on the unwelcome role of an itinerant village urchin. The crossing goes on interminably, like a dream – or rather a nightmare. The minutes are marked off by the rise and fall of German flares. The little rowing boat slides silently over the stagnant water. The two ropes, on which hang the corpses of the Russian scouts Lyakhov and Morozov, float into the frame. In spite of this threat, the little boat carries on its way. German patrols criss-cross the flooded wood, which echoes with their alien, incomprehensible speech. The little figure melts away, lost to sight in the terrifying darkness of the silent tree-trunks . . .

And the story-line breaks off at the very point where the exploits of the brave scout are just about to begin.[5] There is no 'advantage' in this film: everything that happens, happens *between* Ivan's two excursions behind the enemy lines.

In the book the lieutenant stops the story of Ivan half-way through, because he knows no more about what happened to him once he has set off behind enemy lines. *Ivan's Childhood*, however, is a film of motifs rather than action. Its conflicts lie on another, impersonal plane, where 'the invader' is a generalized and somewhat abstract concept and where the faceless silence which swallows Ivan up expresses the meaning more fully than would some concrete clash with the men from the Gestapo.

This explains the finale of the film, which is broader and more allegorical than the short and laconic epilogue to the book.

There is the Reichstag, a symbol of victory, then the German newsreels. Lieutenant Galtsev, the only character in the film to survive, is leafing through files on the Gestapo's victims. The ash from burning papers, the black snow of war, the twisted rolls of barbed wire, the neatly arranged storeys of the prison, the nooses on the gibbets and suddenly, in one of the photographs, the face of Ivan, full of dark hatred, a bruise under one eye. The montage, linking this sequence with the newsreels, with the voluntary suicides and Goebbels's monstrous destruction of his own children, brings to the social – the 'anti-Fascist' – aspect of the film a much broader human resonance.

Ivan's 'story' ends in the Gestapo headquarters, but the film ends elsewhere. Again the smile on the mother's face, the whiteness of the summer sand, the girl and the boy running into the dazzling ripples of a sheet of water and then a black tree, coming into the frame like a sinister sign of warning . . .

In the imagery-system of the film there is a fixed combination of elements which by repeating themselves from scene to scene set up what psychologists would call a 'dynamic stereotype'.[6]

There is the star in the depths of the well that Ivan's mother shows the boy in the midday heat of summer in one of the dreams. Then he is at the bottom of the well, catching it with his hands in the dark water. Or take the graceful white trunks of the silver-birches, filmed from Masha's point of view as she whirls around in the dance, intoxicated with the joy of falling in love. But each such episode, while starting on such a bright and joyful note, suddenly, without any kind of transition, is cut short by catastrophe. The bucket clatters down the well-shaft on to the terrified Ivan; the mother lies dead on the ground. Every dream is the same: a bright beginning and a sudden catastrophic end. And thus it was in waking, too: war burst in on a peaceful day. Ivan's mind has been shaped for all time by the sudden shock of that dislocation, inflicted in childhood, the scar of a violence that will never be effaced. And Masha's waltz also ends with as sudden and terrible an interruption, a sudden clash in the orchestra and a close-up of the two hanging men on 'their' bank.

The film lurches forward from catastrophe to catastrophe. There is hardly any space for the things that we are accustomed to call suffering or resignation. The killing of the mother is a trauma that could never be accepted through tears and grief. War is a trauma that could never become an everyday thing. The violence done to the emotional world of the individual is total. But from this totality, from the near-impossibility of anything normal and human, is born the almost unbearable spiritual thirst for an ideal. From absolute disharmony is born the dream of absolute harmony.

The ideal is continually reborn in each subsequent episode of the film, just as it has been continually destroyed in the previous one. The bright, strange images of childhood in Ivan's dreams are beautiful and untinged by sadness; the solid, rounded, sparkling whiteness of the trunks in the birch grove is unreal, like something from a fairy-tale. The Russian song on the Chaliapin record is filled with a strange majesty and a kind of aching freedom.

For this reason the final sequence in the film, which returns us to the images of childhood, is not merely allegorical, but is an expression of the depth of a need, which grows out of the heart of the film, out of its dislocated imagery. This final sequence is far more than a 'moral', put forward as an 'afterword' by Tarkovsky to cap Ivan's crippled and extinguished childhood. It is an effort of the will, reaching out towards the harmony and wholeness of an ideal for humanity.

Ivan's Childhood shows very clearly the movement away from the prosaic, narrative style of the story to the poetic treatment given to that same material in the film.

It was Viktor Shklovsky in his article 'Poetry and Prose in the Cinema' who first suggested the division of films into 'poetry' and 'prose', explaining that the difference lay not in the subject matter, but in the artist's treatment of it.[7] 'There is a cinema of prose and a cinema of poetry, two different genres; they differ not in their rhythm – or, rather, not only in their rhythm – but in the fact that in the cinema of poetry elements of form prevail over elements of meaning and it is they, rather than the meaning, which determine the composition.'[8]

For us, there is sense in trying another approach to the question: why is it that at some moments in history the cinema feels the need for a poetic treatment of its raw material?

It seems to me that this need is particularly sharply felt during periods of historical change, when our 'normal', accepted notions and perceptions become inadequate in the face of changing realities, and new perceptions have to be developed.

When the conflict raging within the artist reaches that point where a logical or, so to speak, practical expression of it is no longer possible, then he is forced to turn to poetry. In other words, not meaning, but pure composition.

I therefore see the basic trait of the 'poetic' cinema (today, at any rate) in the indirect nature of its statements, as art's attempt to capture that which logic and meaning are incapable of capturing.

This division of the cinema into prose and poetry is, of course, a highly relative distinction.

It could be argued that rigid compartmentalizing is no longer a feature of art today, and that therefore a line of demarcation between realists and poets is as irrelevant today as between realistic and non-realistic theatre, where there used to be such passionate rivalries and arguments. Our perceptions have changed. Nowadays we are witness to *détente* and cross-fertilization to an extent that could be called eclectic, but could also be seen as a synthesis. This is art seeking out new forms of expression for life, and not merely the whim of the artist.

The art critic Efros, who was my teacher, once wrote an essay about the outstanding engraver Favorsky. 'Interesting,' said Favorsky when he read it, 'but nothing like me.' 'And are your portraits like your sitters?' asked Efros.

This 'portrait' of *Ivan's Childhood*, which I wrote under the impact of my first viewing of the film, led to long, unresolved arguments with Tarkovsky. Words like 'poetic', 'symbol', 'metaphor' soon became overworked and, perhaps for that reason, infinitely distasteful to the director. To the end, both in print and in person, he insisted that his cinema was simply 'observation' of reality, that 'the image in cinema is an image of life', and that his favourite art form was the Japanese three-line haiku. These arguments went on intermittently throughout most of Tarkovsky's career and led to innumerable misunderstandings, terminological pitfalls and logical non sequiturs. But that is not the point.

Everything to do with art is personal, from the work of the artist himself right through to the perception of any and every cinema-goer. It is perfectly possible that my 'portrait' of Tarkovsky is as unlike him as his 'portrait' of the war is unlike the war itself.

In this study, I have made an honest attempt at a straightforward 'observation' of the phenomenon of Tarkovsky. '*Feci quod potui*', as the ancients would have said, '*faciant meliora potentes*'. (I have done what I could; let those who are able, do better.)

Part I : Forward to the Past

1 · The Beginning

> That hour of apprenticeship, in all our lives
> Is solemn and essential.
>
> > Marina Tsvetayeva[1]

Andrey Tarkovsky was born on 4 April 1932 in Zavrazhie, near Yurievo in the Ivanovo district, on the Volga. Even though he lived most of his life in Moscow, the house in which he spent his childhood remained for him the 'image' of a family home. This is the house which appears more than forty years later, in *Mirror*. Both his parents had studied at Moscow's Literary Institute. His father, Arseniy Alexandrovich Tarkovsky, one of the most highly regarded modern Russian poets and translators, volunteered for the Front in 1941, where he lost a leg. His fame as a poet was to come later in life, although he has never been 'popular'.

The slim volumes by this poet, who was well past the first flush of youth, fired the imagination of his readers with the density of his thought and the dry, honed-down language in which it was expressed. These volumes were soon to become what is euphemistically known in the Soviet Union as a 'bibliographical rarity'. From his father, Tarkovsky inherited his poetic gift, but not his profession. In fact, the name of Andrey Arsenievich Tarkovsky became well known before that of his father; it was Arseniy who became known as Andrey's father rather than the other way round. Furthermore, Arseniy deserted his family early on, leaving Andrey's mother, Maria Ivanovna Vishnyakova, with two children to bring up. If, therefore, the son could be said to have inherited a spiritual reticence from his father – a reticence that might even deserve the epithet élitist – he inherited it as one of the basic traits of his personality and we can be certain that it was passed down by heredity rather than by example. It is interesting to note that as he grew older, Tarkovsky looked increasingly like his father.

In 1939 he started school in Moscow, but when the war broke out they were evacuated. His mother took Andrey and his younger sister back to her family on the Volga, where he had spent his early childhood.

All these childhood impressions – desertion by his father, their hard life, evacuation, school – were later to find their reflection, one way or another, in *Mirror*. In 1943 the family returned to Moscow, and Tarkovsky to his old school. His school certificate does not bear witness to a strong enthusiasm for any one particular subject. What it does show is a complete lack of any ability or interest in mathematics or the physical sciences and adequate marks in the humanities. Tarkovsky was the product of a traditional artistic upbringing: he studied an instrument for seven years; at the age of thirteen he transferred to a high school with a special emphasis on art, where he seriously took up drawing. All this was gradually building up towards his film career – even in the superficial sense that his first (diploma) film was based upon his recollections of music lessons.

In 1951, however, Tarkovsky entered the Oriental Institute and might have completed his course there were it not for the fact that he concussed himself one day in the gym class.

'When I was studying I often used to think that I had been a little hasty in choosing a career,' Tarkovsky was to state ingenuously in the 'autobiography' which he submitted to the Cinema Institute, 'I know too little of life.' For that reason he did not rush to catch up with all the courses he had missed, but in May 1953 found employment instead as a collector (in other words, an ordinary worker) for one of the scientific institutes on a prospecting expedition to the distant Turukhansky region in the Soviet Far East. He worked for almost a year up and down the wild river Kureika, travelling hundreds of kilometres on foot through the *taiga* and completing a whole album of sketches. 'All this served to confirm my decision to become a film director,' he suddenly says, somewhat surprisingly, in that same 'autobiography'. 'Surprisingly', because the impressions gained from the *taiga*, the expedition, and the romance of it all for an impressionable young man were not to be reflected in his work, aside from student exercises at the Cinema Institute. In the same way, Chekhov's distant journeys to Sakhalin and Ceylon left almost no immediate mark upon his writing. Andrey Tarkovsky's spiritual baggage was acquired during his none-too-happy childhood and was little affected by subsequent external influences.

When he returned from the expedition in 1954, he applied to VGIK and was accepted, having done well in the special tests. It was an auspicious moment, for the time when Andrey Tarkovsky entered the Soviet film world proved to be a watershed in the history of that world. Not long before, film-directing would have had nothing to offer even the greatest genius, simply because the annual production figures were so low. Only just enough films were made to keep the few established directors in work. However, in 1953 the decision was taken to increase film production. In 1954, when Tarkovsky applied to the VGIK, forty-five films – at that time an enormous number – were produced. By 1955 it had already leaped to sixty-six. It was then that Mikhail Romm, who was to be Tarkovsky's teacher, wrote: 'Making few films turned out to be no easier than making many.' The idea of concentrating on a very few films (which was supposed to lead to outstanding quality) turned out to be utopian.

But besides the increase in the quantity of films – which meant an obvious increase in opportunities – there was another fact that would play an important part in Tarkovsky's development: the war generation had arrived at the Institute not long before him. It was this generation that gave birth to the so-called 'VGIK school'. They were young, but not too young to have fought, so they were already experienced and consciously striving to pour that experience into the arts: they burst upon the scene first in poetry, then in prose, theatre and cinema. Although they were still final-year students in the artistic institutes they were already beginning to be published, though their hour of glory was yet to come. It was they who were destined at the end of the fifties and the start of the sixties to bring forth new themes and new means of expression, a new view of life and of the protagonist who lives it. This ferment had already started when Andrey Tarkovsky attended lectures and seminars and worked under Mikhail Romm.[2]

In 1957 two films were made which showed very strongly the trends that were to emerge in this renewal of the Soviet cinema: Segel and Kulidzhanov's *The House Where I Live* and Kalatozov's *The Cranes Are Flying*. *House* was made against the background of neo-realism's innovations, which had captivated and delighted the whole generation. The story of the lives of several neighbours living in the same house unfolds with everyday, lifelike scenes, simple and human and a million miles away from the 'general' and 'monumental' scenes which had until recently been all that graced Soviet screens.

Kalatozov, on the other hand, was a director who had made his name as long ago as 1930 with the documentary *Salt for Svanetia*, written by Sergey Tretyakov; together with the young cameraman Urusevsky he gave a sharply expressive treatment to Rozov's 'chamber' play, filling it out with neo-realist material. *The Cranes Are Flying* was the sensation of the Cannes Film Festival, and suddenly Urusevsky was the cameraman everybody wanted to know. This film ignited Soviet cinema. The discovery of everyday reality paled before the discovery of what could be done with a camera and a screen.

It is tempting to ascribe the artistic quest for which Tarkovsky was to become known to his exposure to Urusevsky's unfettering of the camera in this film. Tarkovsky would always find it easy to assimilate one or other of the fashions that arose in world cinema. His early work, however, demonstrates certain traits of an artistic personality that would remain unchanged throughout his subsequent career.

One of the essays in the VGIK archives is his piece on Sergey Yutkevich's *The Great Warrior Albani Skanderbeg* (1945). This essay shows that his views on the cinema were already formed. The complete break with the former, monumental style of the Soviet cinema was, of course, something that was shared by the whole of Tarkovsky's generation: 'The film gives the impression of being puffed-up and artificial because of the falsely epic and ridiculously monumental quality of the main characters, particularly of Skanderbeg ... The character of Skanderbeg is not based on a careful observation of how the people would have perceived their hero ... He has no depth, no roundness, none of those little details which never escape the attention of the common people.' These remarks might, of course, have been written by any of the students at the VGIK in his time. Later in the essay, however, comes a remark which can be seen as a prologue to the whole of Tarkovsky's career:

> Then follows a trick which probably passes over the heads of the audience. Skanderbeg raises his sword over his vanquished foe, who begs to be finished off. But the next sequence slows down the action: we see a wave rising, growing, and freezing for an instant. If we analyse the single-combat scene, which is given a folk-tale treatment, we will see that this sequence is a metaphor, which in words could be expressed thus: 'as a wave might halt in its relentless rush towards the shore, so the sword of Skanderbeg, raised aloft, froze in his avenging hand'. All very well, but for the audience to penetrate to the essence of this scene would need more time and thought than the director gives it. This does not mean that the audience requires that everything be served-up already chewed and digested. Far from it! *Any idea that is offered to the audience not directly, and that is correctly perceived by the audience in spite of the indirect treatment, will be all the more appreciated by that audience because it calls upon the creative efforts of the audience itself.* [My italics – M.T.] However, allegorical or indirect treatments should never be brain-teasers.

Here, in a nutshell, is encapsulated the whole complex of problems that were to cluster around Tarkovsky's films. Here is his rejection of the mere metaphor. Here, too, is his fundamental emphasis upon the 'creative efforts' of the audience; the indirect treatment which later he was to reject theoretically while in practice resorting to the most blatant 'brain-teasers', without offering the audience even the slenderest of explanations. But, of course, without this complex of problems, Tarkovsky's art simply would not exist.

Also in the VGIK archives is a short study called *The Concentrate* (the only piece of work which refers to his year in the *taiga*). This shows the chief of an expedition waiting on a Yenisei shipping-pier for a boat bearing the concentrates being brought back by a geological party. The visual power of all Tarkovsky's work is already tangible here. The weather, the waiting and the anxiety are all evoked by means of light and sound. The range of lighting effects is highly expressive: the faces of those waiting, for instance, alternately flicker in the beam from the murky lighthouse on the bank and are plunged into darkness. A pale hanging lamp sways on the pier. Indoors, there is a circle of light around the radio-engineer from the lamp on his table. The beam from the lighthouse snatches from the darkness disconnected details of the scene. The monotonous tapping of the morse-transmitter is a background for the gusting of the wind and the crashing of the waves, the threatening sounds of the coming storm. Tarkovsky would always be indifferent to special, cinematic music; but the music of life itself, its sounds and noises, always served him faithfully and with truth. An undertext of alarm is created on the tiny set of this 'workplace' study.

It is no surprise that the greatest influences on him – the decisive ones, it could be said – during his VGIK student days were Buñuel and Bergman. Not because those were the years when these two directors' work was coming into fashion, but because the soil in which these influences could grow was already being cultivated.

Later, the names of Kurosawa and Fellini would be added to the very limited number of contemporary film-makers recognized by Tarkovsky. Theoretically, the nearest to his ideal is probably Bresson, though in practice his work is very different.

Apart from the felicitous circumstances outlined above, there were two other factors at the VGIK in which Tarkovsky was extremely lucky: first, that he studied in the group led by Mikhail Romm and, second, that he found a co-author in Andrey Mikhalkov-Konchalovsky.[3]

At the time, working in pairs was something about which the students had almost no choice, since the facilities were not adequate to provide every student with his own film. Most of those temporary alliances fell apart; although some, like Alov and Naumov, were to become a 'single' film-maker. But in Mikhalkov-Konchalovsky it was a co-author, a like-minded individual whom Tarkovsky found, rather than merely a co-director. As directors they were later to take very different, almost opposite, paths. All that they had in common, cinematically speaking, was their total professionalism.

However, these two most talented students of Mikhail Romm were to conceive and write all their first screenplays (not only their début films) together. They jointly wrote *The Steamroller and the Violin*, then Tarkovsky's *Andrey Rublyov* and Mikhalkov-Konchalovsky's *The First*

Teacher. From the very start, both were imbued with self-confidence: they were the ones who swept into the cinema on the shoulders of the war generation, which had experienced for itself (and learned to give shape and meaning to) the lessons of history, and was well aware of the tasks before it, and of what it could achieve. For the generation of the sixties this new territory no longer remained to be conquered. Their task would be correspondingly easier, though this in turn meant that more would be expected of them in cinematic terms.

And, of course, Romm. Almost all the outstanding directors of today have been his pupils. By the time Romm taught Tarkovsky, he was a classic figure: his first film, *Boule de Suif* was made in the silent era; his were the two classic films about the life of Lenin, *Lenin in October* (1937) and *Lenin in 1918* (1939); *The Dream* was the most visual of all the pre-war films.[4] To a certain extent, his experience was just what his students were reacting against: he was steeped in the narrative cinema of the thirties in its purest form. But Romm was also the most lively and adaptable of the older generation of film-makers. He not only taught his students all he knew but he – and only he, of all his generation – was also prepared to learn from his students. He also lent them money, got them out of scrapes, extended them his protection when they started work at the studio and defended their films – even those which were nothing at all like his own work. He was kind and self-sacrificing. The new qualities which he revealed in his late films *Nine Days of One Year* and *Ordinary Fascism* were due, in large part, to his relationship with these young people. However, not all his students appreciated or reciprocated his selfless concern for them.

Even if Romm's early work was a springboard for Tarkovsky to leap away from, the man himself was the finest of mentors and the most caring of midwives for a young talent.

In 1960 Tarkovsky graduated from the VGIK with top marks and was awarded its Director's Diploma, No. 756038.

2 · *The Steamroller and the Violin*

You, who have lived on earth for me,
My armour and my blood-relations
From Alighieri to Schiaparelli,
I thank you: for how well you burned.

And do not I burn too, and well?
Is it indifference that blinds me
To you, for whom I've lived on earth,
To grass and stars, to butterflies and children?

Arseniy Tarkovsky

Tarkovsky made his first film – to qualify for his diploma – at the Mosfilm Studios in 1960. He wrote the script together with his fellow student Andrey Mikhalkov-Konchalovsky, with whom he was subsequently to conceive and write *Andrey Rublyov*. Between the subject-matter of *The Steamroller and the Violin*, charming as it is, and that of *Andrey Rublyov* the distance is enormous.

The childhood theme of *The Steamroller and the Violin* is an embryonic expression of what was to become Tarkovsky's artistic quest – thematically, stylistically and in many other ways. However, in the light of Tarkovsky's next film, it was to look like an idealization, even a sentimentalization, of childhood.

The story is very simple, developing over a few hours in the yard of an old Moscow apartment house. Up on the fifth floor lives a little boy of six or seven, who is learning the violin. Every morning the 'musician', as the local toughs have christened him, is faced with the enormous task of getting across the yard and through their cruel cross-fire. This morning he is lucky: the yard is being laid with asphalt, and he finds a champion in the driver of the noisy red steamroller. The new friend heaps shame on the toughs (who are, incidentally, sketched somewhat vaguely, simply as a backdrop to the action) and allows the musician a ride on his steamroller. This is the beginning of a friendship between the two 'men', the big and the small. The friendship lasts a few hours, and even turns into a triangle when their developing relationship is jealously observed by the young lady who drives the other (yellow) steamroller, and who tries in a rather crude way to flirt with her colleague.

Strange as it may seem, in this unassuming little story-line we can already find a premonition of the theme of the fate of the artist, which was later to be developed into the vast crowded canvas of *Andrey Rublyov*.

The boy's journey to his music school grows into a whole sequence: he stops by a shop window full of mirrors, and in a mirror sees a woman spill a bag of apples, one of which he will later lay before a tiny girl with a big bow in her hair, waiting solemnly for her lesson.

The lesson itself becomes a clash with the teacher, who fetters his musical imagination to a metronome. It is, however, that same power of imagination that earns the little boy the respect of the working man, from which will come his first taste of self-respect and of respect for art within himself.

At first the older man protects and teaches the boy. On the way back from the lesson the musician leaves his instrument on the steamroller and sets off confidently with his new friend to spend the lunch-hour, during which they then share several adventures.

They see a big thug bullying a little boy, and the workman gives the hero a lesson in courage. Later he stands up for the victim, and for his pains is thumped on the nose by the bully. His reward comes when he is able to return to the little boy the ball which the bully had taken away.

Then they join a crowd of other Muscovites watching an old brick building being demolished with a huge ball and chain. Moscow's far-reaching programme of reconstruction was beginning, and this documentary sequence is a true symbol of the age.

The friends then fall out: the boy, who does everything he can to look like his new workman friend, takes offence at his new friend calling him 'musician' like the gang of toughs do, and flings down on the pavement the loaf of bread that he was carrying for them to share. He has not yet learned either what an honour it is to be called 'musician' or the spiritual value of bread. The workman is horrified at this insult to the loaf of bread: not so many years have passed since the war, when that precious eighth of a loaf of black bread was the only thing that kept people alive, and people knew the moral as well as the material value of bread.

Instinctively, the boy guesses where he went wrong and they become reconciled. Then comes the most important sequence: under a ringing, echoing archway that they have chosen for their lunch-place, the boy takes his half-sized violin from its case, explains to his new friend the little that he himself has learned of how it works, and begins to play. This is the first real lesson in music – and, by inference, in art – that either of them has ever received.

Andrey Tarkovsky never came to regard art as a profession, an amusement or a way of earning a living. For him art was always not only something to devote one's life to, but something any life could worthily be devoted to – a cause. This short film was his first concrete expression of this veneration. Not only the young workman but even the bully, who opens the violin case with rapacious delight, is stopped in his tracks by the sight of the violin, that miracle of civilization, that temple of an unseen world. There may be a certain artificiality about the scene, but it does make transparently clear Tarkovsky's own attitude to the subject matter.

The young workman looks with new respect at the little child's violin with its ornate sounding-holes, and falls silent when he begins to play – playing that is no longer ruled by the strict ticking of the metronome, but regulated by the musician's own inner sense of discipline. And the worker, who must, in his time, have been proud of the calluses on his hands, looks with understanding at the mark left by the violin on the young musician's chin.

Just as, instinctively and without a word being spoken, the boy came to understand the meaning of work and the value of bread, so at this moment the workman comes to understand the great labour and the great power that lie in art. They both learn something, and at once they experience the desire to strengthen their friendship and mutual understanding in the simplest, most mundane way imaginable: arranging to go to the cinema together, to see an old film, *Chapayev*.[1]

Then comes a fatal moment: the boy's strict mother, who understands nothing of the significance of what has happened, simply locks the little musician into the flat, so that the girl is able to carry off the disappointed and offended steamroller-driver into the cinema. We see played out one of those minor, unnoticed dramas whose consequences are far from minor because of the scars they leave upon the human heart.

The last sequence in his diploma film is also unmistakably 'Tarkovskian': the boy, in the red shirt he has put on in honour of the occasion, is running over the fresh asphalt towards the sparkling red steamroller. Dreams can compensate for the harsh traumas of reality.

In this slight film, whose makers were all so young – the writers, the director and the cameraman, Vadim Yusov (who was to work so much with Tarkovsky) – there is already a very clear picture both of the Soviet cinema's quest for altogether new means of expression, and of the individual personalities of the film-makers. That may well be why it has lost none of its freshness.

The most potent evidence of this is the joy of the free camera, released from its fetters. Even if the characters (even the 'toughs') are very obviously actors in make-up, the whole milieu of the film is filled with the play of dappled sunlight, with reflections in mirrors, with glittering water ... all is living, pulsating and redolent of the coming spring. We can feel the play of pent-up energy diffused throughout the film.

From the intriguing locations, like the entrance to the old Moscow apartment house with its coloured-glass panes, to the crooked streets, the resounding archway, the high-ceilinged corridor and the music school with its old, amber-coloured parquet floors and its huge gothic armchair on which the boy clambers, everything is real, familiar – it is Moscow. We are never, however, treated to a still-life, or to a dose of nostalgia. Everything that we are shown is an organic part of a lively, fluid stream of life. A tiny detail – like the boy stopping in front of a shop full of mirrors – is developed into a study of joyful, flickering sunshine, a pattern of reflections of the street, the corner of a building, a trolley, a woman, a golden stream of apples. The asphalt, flooded by a sudden shower, reflects the blinding blueness of the sky. The old archway is full not only of the sound of the little violin, but also of trembling slivers of sunlight, and of blue: the blue of the peeling paint, the darker blue of the workman's overalls, and the deep blue of the velvet that lines the violin-case. The dialogue between the red and the yellow steamrollers and the harmony between the red shirt and the red steamroller against the grey of the wet asphalt create a vibrant, youthful palette. It is not so much the subject matter, or the plot, which is important. For instance, when the two friends become separated, the rain – big friendly drops cascading down on to the crowd that gathers to watch the demolition work – is as important as the event itself. The shower, just like the mirrors in the shop window, becomes a separate sequence in the film, and means just as much as the movement of the plot.

All this was to become an integral part of Tarkovsky's cinema, to multiply therein, transform and mature, as was the hidden note of drama – perhaps even tragedy – in the fact of a relationship interrupted by force, an unintended betrayal.

Strange as it may seem, this undoubtedly successful film led to differences of opinion in the 'Children's and Youth Films' section of the studio where it was made. In this respect it was not only the start of Tarkovsky's career, but also set the tone for his professional life as a whole. The characters and the casting seemed too crude for a children's film, as did the relationship between the young workman and the girl. In fact, with hindsight, they seem at worst unconvincing, too obviously actors. But the substance of the disagreements seems ludicrous and, in any event, they did not extend beyond the confines of the studio. The film won praise in the press when it was released and Tarkovsky soon transferred to another section. But he had already experienced his first trauma and the first testing of his nerve.

While he was still a nobody – not yet the controversial, distinguished Tarkovsky who was to prove himself a unique force – he behaved exactly as he was to behave throughout his life. Uncompromising and undiplomatic, he defended his views on the cinema to anyone and everyone. This was not just one aspect of his prickly character, but an essential feature of his talent. After working on the screenplay for six months, he knew exactly what he wanted on the screen and even in his first film pursued those goals unswervingly. In themselves, the actors were of no particular interest to him, as in the future they were never to be. He could not change his way of seeing, however hard he might try.

'The screen tests are bad,' he told his critics (about screen tests for the adult parts), 'but as for the conception of the film, I have already stated it clearly and I am going to stick to what has already been decided, otherwise we will end up with a twee little children's film . . . It is not the actors who are important, but the idea and the approach. I cannot express anything in a received language.'

Like all young people who became active in the arts after the Twentieth Party Congress, Tarkovsky took some note of the general concerns in the air at this time. But the road he would take lay in a different direction from that of many other directors, such as Chukhrai or Khutsiev. He was striving for his *own* truth and his *own* language. Much water would flow under the bridge before he would express what was truly his *own*, plainly and straightforwardly; but even at the threshold of his career the seed had been sown, and that is why *The Steamroller and the Violin*, for all that it is a short film, and a film for children, deserves to be regarded as an integral part of Tarkovsky's œuvre.

Tarkovsky on *The Steamroller and the Violin*

'The poetry of a thing will come into being only when it is truthful and is given texture. Hardly a word is spoken in the film. For us the most important thing was the scene, the environment. The relationship between this environment and truthfully depicted characters should create the formality I spoke about earlier. We are accustomed to regard something formal as artificial and impenetrable, but I see my formality as having both feet firmly on the ground. I am ready to prove to anyone the rightness of my idea. This way is the only way.'

'This is, in essence, a tragedy. He is traumatized by the boy's not coming to meet him at the cinema and slamming shut the window that had been opened on to a new world.'

'Here the cinema is seen as action. There are no more than thirty-five sentences spoken in the whole film.'

3 · Ivan's Childhood

Tarkovsky's first full-length feature film earned him an international reputation at the very outset of his career. He owed this first success to one of those happy accidents that, if they happen in the theatre, are trumpeted all over the newspapers, while if they happen in the cinema tend to remain behind the closed doors of the studio. In the theatre the classic situation is that the leading actor is suddenly taken ill and the understudy is given a first chance, captures the hearts of the public and wakes up the next morning famous.

When the same kind of thing happens in the cinema industry, it seems much more prosaic. Here are two documents from the studio's archives:

1. Official confirmation that the studio will write off the losses and expenses connected with the full-length feature-film 'Ivan'.

In accordance with the instructions issued by the Director-General of Mosfilm, ref. 466 10/12/60 concerning 'Ivan' (dir. E. Abalov), work has been stopped because the scenes shot on location were deemed unsatisfactory ... They cannot be used. The expenses incurred to date on 'Ivan' will have to be written off.

2. Instructions from the Director-General of Mosfilm, Comrade Surin, for a return to work on the film 'Ivan', 16/6/61.

In accordance with the approach made by Creative Section No. 1,[1] work is to be resumed on the film from 15/6/61. The shooting script must be confirmed by the head of the Section by 30/6/61. The work is to be undertaken by Tarkovsky (director), Yusov (camera) and Cherniaev (design).

This was how Tarkovsky was handed the subject matter for his next film, like being bequeathed a legacy riddled with debts. Even if the financial losses occasioned by Abalov (a young director of Tarkovsky's generation whose name has since faded into oblivion) were not transferred to his successor, the moral wrong incurred had to be put right. Tarkovsky had to film faster and more cheaply than usual, and there was no more room for mistakes. The normal trial-and-error period allowed to any beginner had already been frittered away by his predecessor.

The sequences shot by the first crew have not survived, and therefore it is not possible to measure the distance covered by Tarkovsky in the short time available to him. But a folder of pictures for screen-tests has been preserved, and on the basis of these we can calculate the degree to which the film is the original work of Tarkovsky.

One set of photographs is of actors tested for the part of Ivan. Among the five faces there are very young boys, some older ones, peasant faces and more intellectual ones, fair and dark boys. But not one of them bears any resemblance to that expression of inner conflict, that quality of apartness, that the director found in the face of Moscow schoolboy Kolya Burlyaev. The boy chosen by Abalov has an attractive face, in some ways perhaps more 'typical' than Kolya's, but an ordinary face. Tarkovsky's Ivan not only lives a strange and harrowing life in the shadow of a lonely death by torture, but he is conceived from the very start as an unusual individual. For all his extreme youth, he is a personality who would stand out in any crowd – in fact, an *alter ego* for the director and author of the film.

Tarkovsky's overwhelming desire from the very first to be the author of the film on an equal footing with the author of the story (or, more precisely, the *sole* author) is apparent from his clashes with another, equally strong personality and equally stubborn talent – that of the story's creator and the prototype of its protagonist, Vladimir Bogomolov.

There had already been a great deal of argument over the script, starting at least a year before Tarkovsky came to work on the film in August 1960.

Ivan, a novella written in 1957, was already a classic and had been translated into more than twenty languages when it attracted the attention of the experienced screen writer M. Papava, who completely rewrote the story for the cinema. The first half of his screenplay tells the story of Ivan, the little scout: in the second half, Lieutenant Galtsev, who imagined that Ivan was dead, unexpectedly meets him in a train. Ivan is married, and his wife is expecting a child. In this way the writer completely transformed the basic theme of the story, giving its hero the gift of a life – in fact, he even changed its title to 'A Second Life'.

This rode roughshod over the logic of life itself: at about that time there was an article in the youth newspaper *Komsomolskaya Pravda* about the young scouts who had helped the armies on the Dneiper in 1941. The article ended with the words, 'Where are you now, young heroes? Come forward!' Bogomolov (himself a former scout) rang the newspaper. Nobody had come forward. Ivan's contemporaries were all dead, to the last man.

It also rode roughshod over the literary source: Ivan was a tragic hero, and could never be anything else. No one was therefore surprised when Bogomolov stepped in and insisted forcefully that the story should return to its original form.

Because of his jealous campaign for the integrity of his original story, it *is* perhaps surprising that he agreed at once to the main innovation which Andrey Tarkovsky proposed in his first memorandum as director: Ivan's dreams – an invasion of images from another, more natural life into the harsh reality of war.[2]

The introduction of the dreams transfers the narrative initiative to Ivan: the war as a whole is shown through the eyes of a younger generation. The gap between generations sometimes seems unimportant during periods in our history, but at other times becomes acute when there is a complete change in attitudes over the space of only a few years. Bogomolov was a part of that 'war generation' which in the cinema was forcefully represented by Chukhrai, with his *The Forty-First*, *The Ballad of a Soldier* and *The Clear Sky*. They had arrived at the front little more than boys, and by the end of the war they were officers, professionals who had matured rapidly in those two or three years. Tarkovsky was not much younger, but what attracted him in the subject matter of *Ivan* was not so much the achievements of the young hero as the terrible significance of what they masked: the destruction of the bright and natural world of childhood, and Ivan's violent and tragic coming of age. He wanted to change the title right from the start, adding the word 'childhood'.

It may be that Bogomolov did not at once appreciate the complete change of structure that the inclusion of the seemingly innocuous dream sequences would bring about. All the arguments (some of them extremely heated) that took place between the author and director were centred not on the dreams, but on the way in which the everyday reality of the war was depicted. The writer insisted on the precise date, 1943, and on the professionalism of the scouts, whose approach to their work was, as he said, 'head and shoulders above that of the ordinary soldier'; he also explained that under the command of young lieutenants like Galtsev would be hundreds of older men – men with their own families. Many of his practical proposals, especially textual ones, were accepted and proved invaluable, but the director remained deaf to anything he wanted on the military side – the supermen of espionage were of no interest to Tarkovsky at all. Everything had to be seen through Ivan's eyes, and for him war was nothing but a hateful dislocation of the natural world of childhood. From this flows the intensely expressive image-structure of the film, which at the time seemed to be an integral trait of Tarkovsky's work, even though he never returned to that style again.

For Tarkovsky the clash with Bogomolov forced him at a very early stage in his career consciously to take a stand not simply as 'director' (as he was referred to in all the official Mosfilm documents) but as 'author-director', which he became once and for all. 'We have as much right to our creative individuality as you have to yours,' said the young, unknown director to the young, already established writer. To appreciate the boldness of this remark in its context, it is important to remember the strict hierarchy within which the arts in Russia have always been regarded, and the fact that literature still ranks much higher in prestige than the cinema.

This Tarkovsky was determined to challenge.

Throughout the world, however, this was a period of growing self-awareness and self-confidence for the cinema. The recognition of the medium as an art form – due in large part to the Soviet montage pioneers – lay far behind in the twenties. The triumph of neo-realism in the early fifties led to a new marriage of the technical advances in sound-recording with the expressive power of the screen in the following decade. These were the years of the director as artist and of what has come to be known in the West as '*auteur*' cinema. Tarkovsky was to keep faith in this respect with the heroes of his youth, Vigo and Buñuel, and with his admired older contemporaries, Bergman, Fellini and Bresson. Even though the status of the director as author has fluctuated since the sixties, there was never any question of Tarkovsky's role as the '*auteur*' of his films.

Another Tarkovsky quality became apparent during those early days of *Ivan's Childhood*: his thorough professionalism. The crew went on location to Kanev, on the Dneiper, to where the events recalled by Bogomolov really happened. Even those scenes which at first were to be shot in the studio – the battalion field station and intelligence HQ – were created on location. Only one sequence, Kholin and Masha's meeting in the birch-grove, was shot near Moscow. Tarkovsky was to return to this same evocative birch-grove when filming *Andrey Rublyov*.

Although production timetables are usually more lenient when filming with children, the crew managed to work faster than average. The records show that an average of 40.7 usable metres per day were shot in the studio, and 22.8 on location. They had to endure bad weather, with much rain. The 'hero' was not particularly robust, so his mother had to take time off work (she was an engineer) to care for him during the shooting. By 18 January 1962 shooting was finished. On 30 January Tarkovsky showed the first roughcut of the film. On 3 March it was approved. It had cost 24,000 roubles less than the original budget, so Tarkovsky had partly made up for the losses incurred by his unsuccessful predecessor. In the statistical breakdown of the finances which usually follows the completion of a Soviet film, there was mention of 'the work of the young director, who always knew what to shoot, and had a thorough, all-round grasp of the technical aspects'. At the time, it seemed a result of his thorough training. Now, after looking through the various versions of the screenplay proposed by the director, what is striking is the detailed precision, right from the start, not only of the scenes taken directly from the original story, but of the director's own dream-sequences as well. He knew from the very first draft exactly what would go into the final version.

Ivan's Childhood was the Soviet entry in the Venice Film Festival. The shock experienced in the small viewing-room at the Film-Makers' Union was repeated: the film returned with the Grand Prix, the Golden Lion.

That was the dawn of the golden age of film festivals: when they made front-page news and shook the world with discoveries of new subjects, new names and aesthetic innovations. The young Tarkovsky was seen as part of a new 'Soviet school' which had emerged with *The Cranes Are Flying* and *The Ballad of a Soldier*. Immediately after the Venice Film Festival, he received a prize in San Francisco for direction. This thirty-year-old beginner had established himself almost overnight among the élite of world cinema, a position that he would never lose.

Tarkovsky on *Ivan's Childhood*

'Ivan is a child consumed by an adult passion. He loses his childhood in the war and dies because he lived like a grown-up. The whole film must be built around the boy's character, but there must be sequences which show clearly that he is a *child*. There is one concrete detail in the story – Ivan playing at war – which shows this in the most harrowing way.'

'Everything in this film must be profound, terrible and true. There is no room here for romance and adventure. The boy must not be the pride and joy of the regiment, he must be its grief. They all suffer when he goes "over the river". It is the boy's adult passion that makes them suffer with him.'

'I am simply in love with the subject. I was his age when the war began. His situation is that of my generation.'

'You must not miss the theme of Russia, in the texture and character of the locations. We have to bring out the problem of the Russian character, and its psychology.'

4 · *Andrey Rublyov*

Peals of bells, clanging, ringing . . .
Resounding chimes . . .
For
You artists
Of all times!

        Andrey Voznesensky[1]

The white stone wall of a church; against it, the patchy body of a hot-air balloon, sewn together from different-coloured sheepskins and pieces of leather looks even uglier. Smoke rises from the fire that is to lift up into the sky this clumsy fifteenth-century flying machine. A horse crops the grass by a slow-flowing river. On the river a peasant is rowing a boat, unhurried, carrying the seat on which he will take his premature first flight over the still-deserted Russian landscape, hardly yet touched by the artefacts of man. There is a hum of voices and an astonished, joyful cry: 'I'm flying!' The whole earth with its churches, rivers and herds unfolds, then spins like a globe, beneath the feet of this antediluvian air-traveller. Suddenly the ground lurches upwards and our ears are filled with the bubbling of water fast filling the deflated, formless sac which a moment before had been a flying-machine . . .

    This is the airborne prologue with which Tarkovsky begins his film about the great Russian icon-painter Andrey Rublyov. Little is known of the historical Rublyov, and the little that we *do* know is certainly not enough on which to build a biography. This could, of course, have given a biographer unlimited poetic licence. But Tarkovsky and Mikhalkov-Konchalovsky had no such intentions.

'Rublyov's life-story is a complete mystery,' they wrote in their synopsis of the screenplay, 'and we have no intention of unravelling the riddle of his life. We wish to see, through the eyes of a poet, that wonderful and terrible age when the great Russian nation was taking form and shape and coming into its own.'

Rublyov's time was also a time of internecine struggles between the princes, of suffering beneath the Tartar yoke, and of many lesser sorrows and troubles. The two Andreys, Tarkovsky and Mikhalkov-Konchalovsky, identified closely with the poem 'Master-Craftsmen', which had brought fame in 1958 to a third Andrey, Voznesensky:

> Giving birth in bare ravines,
> While riderless horses gallop and cry.

For the sixties' generation, art was a sacred act:

> Art was raised
> From torture, execution . . .
> As it rose, it beat against
> The Moabite stone . . .

'A book is an action', as the hero of *Mirror* was later to say.

They saw the harmony of Rublyov's frescos as a triumph over the disharmony of life itself. There were already biographical films, in abundance, in those post-war years, from Eisenstein's *Ivan the Terrible* on the one hand (the second part was released only in 1957) to all the clichéd stereotypes on the other. Little wonder that young film-makers, striving to bring out all the complexity of their country's history, should choose to do so by means of what might be called an 'anti-biographical' film.

Thus, they saw Andrey Rublyov as 'protagonist' rather than 'hero' of the film. His role in the action is passive rather than active: that of an observer, meditating upon what happens, and if he *is* involved, it is only in a secondary way since his purpose in the film is something other. Different characters are pushed forward one after another into the spotlight; like *La Dolce Vita*, the film is a series of episodes through which passes Andrey Rublyov, artist and monk, sometimes curious, sometimes joyful, sometimes recoiling in horror or sharing in the suffering.[2]

And in fact, as in Rublyov's most famous fresco, the protagonist is not one artist but a 'Trinity'. There are three monks, three icon-painters, and three very distinctive characters: Andrey, his mentor and companion Daniil Chorny, and his envious rival Kirill. The artist is therefore depicted in this three-in-one group comprising: the experienced, somewhat conservative tradition (Daniil); the solitary but determined seeker (Andrey); and the passionate but fruitless revolt of the untalented (Kirill). The relationship between the three monks, who have left their monastery to set off together for Moscow on foot, sets the theme into which the structure of the film will be woven: the artist and time.

In the various episodes, however, this theme is fragmented, multiplied, and refracted through the lives of other artists, building up to a powerful cycle of frescos of Russian life under the unifying title of *Andrey Rublyov*.

The action spans a quarter of a century. The film contains eight episodes, each with its own separate title and date. The first, 'The Mummers', is set in 1400, and the last, 'The Bell', in 1423.

In spite of this rigid demarcation by titles and dates, the structure of the film seems fluid not only because it spans the years of wandering of Andrey Rublyov and his comrades, but also because there are no beginnings or ends in the life it depicts. Life flows on, pausing here or there at this or that individual or event, drawing in Andrey, too, at the circumference of these events.

It is to escape from the rain, for instance, that the three monks take shelter in a hut where a wandering mummer is entertaining the peasants by making fun of the boyars' nobility. The entertainment has been going on for some time, and the mummer is tired of making jokes, while the peasants are tired of laughing. Entertaining is hard work and when he falls exhausted they revive him with an onion and a mug of home-brewed beer. They serve him with respect: they all know what it is to work to the point of exhaustion. There is no amusement in the entertainer's eyes, or in those of the peasants: their experience of life is very much the same.

The camera pans unhurriedly, giving us time to take in the rough-hewn logs with which the hut is built, the tiny apertures of the windows, the crude benches, the peasants in their hempen shirts, the ragged children on the floor, the cart and harness in the doorway, the grey rain and the mud outside in which other peasants are fighting, the horse, unhitched from the cart, grazing in the distance, Kirill slipping quietly out of the hut into the rain . . . The physical milieu of the film is exceptionally solid and lived-in, expressive without being fussy or antiquarian. It confers authenticity on all that takes place within it.

Being a mummer, being an entertainer, is not merely a job, it is also a calling, a free artistic vocation. Wringing the sweat from his shirt in the doorway, he suddenly crows like a cock, horses around and hangs head-down from the lintel of the door.

Then the prince's forces appear, jumping off their horses and shouting to the mummer. He freezes for a moment in the doorway, arms flung out like a crucifix, then they seize him and, dispassionately but skilfully, slam his body against the wood. He falls unconscious. They deftly destroy the instrument he was playing, then fling his senseless body over a saddle and are gone. All eyes are on the monks, who hurry out of the hut into the emptiness of the flat plains, where the riders are moving in single file along the opposite bank of the river.

An even more terrible vision of the artist's fate is seen in 'Last Judgement, 1408'. Here it is not a case of a humble mummer being beaten up, but an attack upon a whole group of proud and skilful master-craftsmen, builders and stonemasons. The proud, white-stone cathedral of Vladimir is waiting to be frescoed, the prince's children playing innocently on the porch; we see the Grand Prince of Vladimir; craftsmen are making their way through the beautiful summer forest to work at the invitation of the prince's younger brother. No one suspects a thing. Suddenly, the woods are full of prancing horses. One rider clamps a mason's head to his horse's side with his knee, and with a swift movement puts out his eyes. The riders surround the group of craftsmen, and it is all over in a moment. Instead of cheerful voices, the forest is filled with their heart-rending cries, their shirts white shapes crawling among the bushes – that will teach a younger brother to dare compete with the older.

These bloody memories haunt Andrey as he stands before the blinding-white interior wall of the cathedral he is to decorate with a fresco of the 'Last Judgement'. Tormented by the experience, he fouls the virginal purity of the wall with an ugly splash of black paint, a stain of despair. Suddenly a mute, simple-minded girl bursts into tears at such ugliness.

In spite of all he has witnessed, it is not the harrowing aspect of the 'Last Judgement' that will finally take root in Andrey's imagination; although he keeps his team of painters waiting for days, it is not in order to work himself into a fever of apocalyptic vision.

The authors of the film see the artist's achievement in his ability to transcend life's horrors: the 'Last Judgement' emerges as a triumph of humanity. It is not the fear of the Lord that he wishes to put into the minds of men, but trust in man; and so he paints not sinners writhing in torment, but human beauty.

The 'Last Judgement' episode is preceded by three others, entitled 'Theophanes the Greek, 1405', 'The Passion According to Andrey, 1406' and 'Feast-Day, 1408'. Through the whole film runs the thread of a long-running dispute between Andrey and his older contemporary, the famous Theophanes. The historic original of this character really was a Greek, and many Russian churches still boast the stern, tragic countenances of his saints and prophets. Theophanes, passionate and impatient, is given more individuality in the film, more personality, than Andrey. It is when the Greek rebuffs the learned, but untalented, pretensions of Kirill that the latter decides to leave the monastic life. It is Theophanes, too, who invites Andrey to work alongside him, revealing the differences in their outlook. Andrey counters the brooding quality of the Greek's art with his own perception of Golgotha: set in the gentle, snowy hills of Russia, with the prince's forces instead of Roman legionaries, peasants in hempen shirts instead of the people of Jerusalem, a small brown dog running ahead of the procession and, most important, a willing victim to redeem these ignorant and innocent people, a meek Christ walking barefoot through the snow of a village street. This is how Tarkovsky perceives 'The Passion According to Andrey'.

Later, nightfall finds the group of painters on Midsummer's Eve near a village in the forest where the inhabitants have been converted forcibly to Christianity. Fearful of the prince's retribution, they celebrate their older, pagan rituals in secret. On this night of magic, torches flicker among the trees and bushes; the mist rises from the river; there is a sound of muffled whispering, song and laughter; naked girls and boys come together from far and wide for their ritual coupling. Andrey is drawn into this feast of freedom celebrating human flesh and earthly love, and nearly becomes the pagans' victim when they take fright at his monk's habit. Later, in the misty dawn, the floating coffin of a ritual dummy nears the icon-painters' boat, and they witness the prince's men hunting down the pagans, catching a man while a naked woman, her hair flowing free, escapes and swims swiftly to the other bank of the broad, slow river. It is from this pagan village that they acquire the simple-minded girl who liberates Andrey and whom he will take with him everywhere he goes.

At first the authors of the film had entertained the idea of showing the monk sinning with a woman, but later they decided against this, although they searched carefully through the faces in the 'Last Judgement' fresco to find one of a woman who might have been loved by the artist. In the end it is the simpleton, one of the many holy fools of God who abounded in Russia at the time – a natural, charming and guileless creature – who comes to symbolize human innocence for Andrey, and this is why her instinctive horror and tears at the ugly black splash in the Cathedral of the Dormition sets the final tenor for Rublyov's treatment of the Last Judgement. It is also the attack on her by the Tartars that brings Andrey to commit that other mortal sin, murder, after which he takes his vow of silence.

The next episode, 'Attack, 1408', is one of the climactic sequences of the whole film. The film's authors clearly regarded the internecine struggles of the princes as far more terrible than the yoke of the Tartars, and it is the same younger brother of the Grand Prince who urges the Tartars to attack the great city of Vladimir. The idea of 'a choice of evils' is embodied by having one and the same actor play both brothers, showing that neither is justified in this feud, for which the people pay in blood and suffering.

The attack begins with the meeting of the Tartars and the Prince's men, first within the same compositional frame, shot on the diagonal: in the upper half of the frame, on the far bank of the river, stand the Russians, while the horned helmets of the Tartars ride into view in the lower half. Then comes the crossing: on a shaky wooden structure, a handsome young Russian prince stands on a white horse and a handsome young Tartar khan on a black one. A Tartar soldier falls into the water and the Russian prince throws him a rope. The prince is embarrassed, while the khan shows his white teeth in laughter, for he somewhat despises his richly dressed ally, perfidiously leading him on towards a Vladimir undefended in the absence of the Grand Prince.

This beautiful sequence is followed by one of purest horror. The undefended city is stormed and destroyed, by fire and sword. It is the self-extermination of the Russian people.

Tarkovsky films the battle with the same authenticity as the earlier scenes of everyday life, both in the crowded, disjointed detail and in the breadth of the overall view. Later, in one of the versions of the screenplay for *Mirror*, he was to introduce a theory for the depiction of battle, a fragment from a treatise by Leonardo da Vinci; but here, any theory he might hold is embodied in the work itself. The screen is full of details: the ladders of the storming forces, a short struggle on the city walls, a torch with which a Tartar sets fire to a wooden roof, a Vladimir peasant hoisting a Tartar aloft on a bear-hunting spear, two Tartars dragging along a Russian girl . . . one of the prince's men, in armour, chasing an unarmed fellow countryman, a horse plunging down from the wall . . . a ram smashes in the gigantic doors of the Cathedral of the Dormition, where the frescoes are barely dry . . . a sudden rush of horsemen into the cathedral, where the people of Vladimir are praying on their knees in terror . . . the soot-blackened, defaced Rublyov frescoes, the businesslike sacking of the cathedral, with the soldiers dragging away the gold they have torn down from the cupolas, and the torture of Patrikei, the cathedral's treasurer . . . Rublyov's useless pupil Thomas is pierced by an arrow at the end of the battle and falls slowly into the stream, like an angel with one wing . . . and Andrey himself – when he sees one of the prince's men dragging away the deaf-and-dumb girl, he brings an axe crashing down on the man's head.

And afterwards, more telling details: the smoking ruins of the cathedral; corpses; the simple-minded girl dreamily plaiting the hair of a dead woman; snow swirling inside the walls, their cupolas lost; and Andrey, raging beside the scorched fresco with Theophanes. Andrey's face is dark and flushed while Theophanes's is drained and bloodless. He is of course long since dead, but appears to Andrey in his delirium to resume their long-standing argument once again. This time, however, Theophanes takes Andrey's side and reaffirms Andrey's shaken faith. It is to him that Andrey confesses his sin and his doubts, and offers his vow of silence. A horse comes through the open-swinging doors and picks its way among the corpses. Snow – its presence inside the church is an image of destruction and disaster.

The next episode, 'Silence', is the only one without a date. We do not know how long Andrey's creative silence lasted; in the film it is fifteen years. But just as the 'Attack' is a broader and more complex image than merely the depiction of one battle (even though actual details, for instance the torture of Patrikei, were taken from chronicles of the time), so the 'Silence' is also the silence of an impoverished life – but a life that is quietly gathering strength for the coming rebirth.

We have already referred to the reality and authenticity of the physical milieu in which the film takes place. Unlike the quoted Voznesensky poem, with which the film has much in common, there is nothing in the film that might be described as outlandish. One thing in Tarkovsky that always strikes the viewer is the unfailing power of his imagination, directed towards what Kracauer terms the 'redemption of physical reality'.[3] In this respect he has no equal. With the exception perhaps of *Ivan's Childhood* and the particular effect that he was striving for there, the director's imagination did not lean towards either the Eisensteinian compression or the Dovzhenkian pantheistic hyperbole which were the foundation stones of Soviet art cinema. The slow-flowing, swollen rivers with their low banks, the moated meadows with grazing unsaddled horses, the low hills, a land that is still half-empty, hardly touched by the hand of man, reminds us rather of the lines of Aleksandr Blok:

> Russia, girded by rivers,
> Surrounded by wastes . . .

This is the Russia of the fifteenth century that we find in the film.

Here the life of the spirit flows against a background of the everyday concerns of a farming people: the cattle are being herded home; a peasant cart meanders behind, piled high with firewood cut in preparation for the winter. The monks in the monastery, including the icon-painters, are cutting wood, carrying water, moving cabbages and sorting the shrivelled apples from a bad harvest. And it is back here, back to the shadow of the wooden walls and towers of the monastery, that Kirill, frantic after his escape to the secular world, returns – life is calmer here. And it is here that we see the simple-minded girl, driven by hunger, set off to be a Tartar's wife. Over in the Tartar camp there is more to eat, and the Tartar raid falls into perspective less as an enemy attack than as another prosaic episode in the unfolding history of coexistence. It is no longer clear whether the Horde will swallow up Russia, or Russia swallow the Horde that has scattered across its plains. Silence . . .

The last episode – dated much later, 1423 – bears an almost symbolic title: 'The Bell'. Although in *Andrey Rublyov* Tarkovsky avoids too-obvious symbolism, there is something about the moist spring warmth in the earth, with patches of snow melting here and there, the bubbling streams, the canvases laid out on the black ground to be primed, that builds up into a powerful chord of awakening.

The village to which the prince's men come in search of a bell-caster is empty: those whom the princes and the Tartars did not take were finished off by disease and sickness. All that is left is one pathetic, skinny boy, living in a ruined hut with no more than a ragged sheepskin to his name. This boy, Boriska, volunteers to cast the bell (claiming that his father left him the secret), and becomes the true hero of this last and most impressive episode. He, too, is played by Kolya Burlyaev.

Among the film's many representations of 'the artist', Boriska represents frenzied determination, single-mindedness and devotion to a God-given talent. As Voznesensky puts it, 'the lightning of your talent burned you to ash'. Boriska invents the story about the 'secret', but the image and the sound of the bell were already hammering at his soul long before the prince's men came.

This small, hungry stutterer with his boyish voice takes on a task that would daunt any adult. So frenzied is his faith in himself as he issues commands to the experienced casters, forcing them to go back again and again to find just the right clay, that they cannot help obeying his sheer spiritual authority, unsupported by any guarantee of success. Even the prince's chancellery is powerless before him.

Strange as it may seem at first glance, the prototype for the kind of hero portrayed by Kolya Burlyaev dates from the beginning of the thirties, during the first days of industrialization and the early Five Year Plans. The same frenzied and selfless approach, risking their own lives and those of others, expecting neither privileges nor recompense for their efforts, was to be found among those captains of the first Five Year Plans, the comrades-in-arms of Ordzhonikidze, the 'Iron Commissar'.[4] To create an industry almost out of nothing, they needed nothing more than society's sanction and the feeling of right on their side.[5]

At first Tarkovsky meant to give the part of Boriska not to Burlyaev, but to a strange and gifted young man called Seriozha Chudakov. However, he grew too big for Boriska while the film was in preparation. Since the director was none too pleased by the somewhat abrasive attitude of his young actor, Kolya's presence may well have been a good thing for the film as a whole. (Kolya was later to train as a film director in his own right, and gained a prize at the Oberhausen Film Festival for his diploma film).

In the characters played by Kolya Burlyaev, the qualities of self-sacrifice and of apartness were intensified by his youth and physical frailness, all of which underscored his spiritual strength.

The enormous size of the casting-pit for the bell, with people crawling over it like flies, gives physical form to this contrast. Exhausted, his torn sheepskin barely covering his naked body, Boriska is as ruthless with others as he is with himself: he orders his best and only friend, brought specially from the village, to be flogged to show the others what will happen if they make a mistake, and the work speeds up to the sound of his cries and sobs.

As a result of this frenzied activity, the bell takes shape. As it shrugs off its clay mould, rising huge and still hot, covered with bronze designs, little Boriska presses himself against its warm side, against the convex picture of St George trampling the dragon beneath his horse's hooves.

It is not Kirill's arguments that persuade Rublyov to break his vow of silence, but this ecstatic celebration of awakening, brought into being by this skinny, childish figure. Impressive clerical figures arrive to bless the bell; the prince appears, surrounded by his attendants and emissaries of foreign powers (the work goes on against the background of melodious Italian speech), and the bell rises up, still covered in scaffolding, trusses and ropes. Suddenly its powerful brazen voice rings out over the heads of the prince's foreign guests, over the excited human ant-hill, and over Boriska himself who is weeping furiously, clutching the heaped-up earth. It is at this moment that the monk, no longer young, leans down to him and pronounces his first words since he took the vow of silence: 'We'll go off together, you and me. You'll cast bells, I'll paint icons. That will give people something to celebrate.' And suddenly, over the sound of the bell and the smoke of the fire, float the faintest, faded colours: red, yellow and white. Slowly emerge the cracks in the plaster of an old fresco, different parts of the vestments of a saint – a girdle, a mitre or a sleeve; then a landscape and a graceful little town, painted in the 'reverse-perspective' technique: trees, animals, a prince on a white horse, angels and the countenance of the Almighty; and finally, piece by piece, it builds up to the Trinity, in a tender harmony of colours and angelic faces. Then again: rain, a slow-moving river, and horses in the rain, grazing peacefully by the water . . .

So ends *Andrey Rublyov*.

Andrey Rublyov could be seen as the first independent creation of the young director. His application to make it was submitted in 1961, even before he made *Ivan's Childhood*. The contract was signed by 1962; on 18 December 1963 the film treatment he submitted was passed; and on 24 April 1964 permission was at last given for the director to start work.[6]

Just as Boriska's bell was first revealed with pieces of mould, scaffolding and ropes still clinging to it, so in the first synopses of the screenplay we can still see contemporary, autobiographical, concerns adhering to this emerging project for a historical film. We find, for instance, the theme of foreign invasion, which was first realized in *Ivan's Childhood*. An episode where the Russian women and girls sacrificed their hair (the place where the Tartars cut off their long plaits is still called 'The Maidens' Field') was one which gripped Tarkovsky's imagination, and he referred directly to the 'heaps of women's hair' in the Auschwitz museum.

The complexity of the artist's relationship with his own art was another of the young authors' concerns: Rublyov became a witness to the deification of his own, unsuccessful icon of the Mother of God, which only by chance he had failed to destroy. As they worked on the screenplay, however, the historical aspect squeezed out these more personal concerns. The structure of the script was simplified: at first, the story of the 'Last Judgement' fresco served as a framework; Andrey was seen running through a field, and episodes from the past flashed before his eyes. Then Tarkovsky turned away from this subjective approach, preferring to model his work on that of an objective chronicler of the times.

He long nurtured the hope of filming the decisive battle where the Russians fought the Tartars at Kulikovo Polye in 1380, but it would have cost 100,000 roubles. Instead, he worked out a cheaper and artistically more interesting idea: showing the morning after the battle. By the time the script was printed, this had become the prologue to the film.[7] He liked the scene so much that when it was not used for *Andrey Rublyov*, he tried to film it as part of *Mirror*. Paradoxical as it might seem, the lack of the Kulikovo battle sequence, ruled out by a cost estimate that was already very high even without it, was later to hold up the film's progress.

Apart from these few changes, however, even the earliest versions of the script give a very full account of the actual content of the eventual film. Many details were cut down, pushed into the background, or left on the cutting-room floor: the 'Maidens' Field' episode, for instance, remained only as a faint echo. 'The 'flying peasant' episode became completely detached from the story of Rublyov (at first he was to have helped the peasant, then to have buried him and kept his death a secret from the people) and emerged as a self-contained prologue. Overall, however, the 'crystalline structure' of the film, as always with Tarkovsky, remained intact.

Preparations started on 9 September 1964, and filming lasted more than a year, until November 1965. The first rough-cut was ready on 25 August 1966. At the end of 1966 the film was shown to the Moscow film world, which was stunned. Never had such a teeming, complex, crowded panorama of medieval Russian life been seen on Soviet screens. The authors' historical ideas were much criticized. The tragic violence of their conception seemed unjustified to many. The fifteenth century could just as easily have been depicted as the age of a nationwide flowering of Russian culture. Others criticized the film's length.

Even the director realized that the editing needed to be sharper: he shortened the film immediately by nearly 400 metres (the first version was 5,642 metres long, the second only 5,250). Over the next few weeks Tarkovsky cut a further 174 metres (the distribution copy was 5,076 metres).

Tarkovsky's opponents accused the film of a lack of optimism, a lack of humanism, a failure to show the known resistance to the Tartar yoke (no Kulikovo battle, for instance), a surfeit of violence and nudity and an over-complexity of form. The film was not entered for the Cannes Film Festival, which would have been the natural successor to the triumph at Venice of *Ivan's Childhood*.

Tarkovsky was too firmly convinced of his rightness, as an artist, meekly to accept the point of view of his opponents:

> I would be so bold as to call myself an artist [he wrote to the then chairman of the State Committee for the Cinema], and more than that, a Soviet artist. My two guiding beacons are what I can create, and life itself. When it comes to problems of form, I seek new ways forward. This is always arduous and can potentially lead to conflict and unpleasantness, so that I cannot count on being able to live a cosy little life in a nice flat, untroubled by anything. What is

demanded of me is courage, and in this respect, I will try not to betray the trust that you have shown me.

In fact Tarkovsky's films always met with the same kind of reception because they defied a purely monothematic appreciation. They are hard to 'understand', and therefore the immediate inference is that the audience, too, will understand nothing.

When, however, with the passage of time the cinema catches up with the director, his films then seem perfectly accessible and even good box-office material. The innovatory qualities that formerly appeared so shocking are dissolved into the advancing stream of cinematic form.

Just as the Romans used to say *'Habent sua fata libelli'*, we could easily say that films, too, have their own fate. *Andrey Rublyov* was released five years later on 19 October 1971. Ten years had passed since the very first application. Ten years, and the film seemed in no way dated, in spite of the speed with which things move in the world of the cinema. The only change was that the film had ceased to be 'difficult' – a judgement in which its author, too, concurred. To this day it remains in no way dated.

Tarkovsky on *Andrey Rublyov*

'One of the most important conventions of the cinema is that a cinematic image can be embodied only in the factual, natural forms of life as we see and hear it. What we show has to be naturalistic. When I speak of naturalism, I do not mean this in its negative sense as a dwelling on the less pleasant aspects of reality, but in its role in the sense-perception of the cinematic image.

'Dreams depicted on the screen must consist of elements as sharply visual as the natural forms of life itself.'

'We are now finishing work on a film about Andrey Rublyov. The action takes place in the fifteenth century, and we discovered just how difficult it is to imagine "what it was like". We had to base our work on anything we could find: architecture, oral history and iconography.

'If we had decided to stick to a re-creation of the artistic tradition, to the world of paintings of that time, then we would have given birth to a stylized and artificial medieval Russian reality . . . One of the things we were aiming for in our work was to re-create the *real* world of the fifteenth century for the audiences of today; in other words, to show that world in such a way that they could really *feel* what would otherwise be a shadowy world of museums and monuments. In order to achieve the truth of direct experience, what could be called a "physiological" truth, we had to break away from other truths which are archaeological or ethnographic in character.'

'The film is about Rublyov . . . But for us its true spiritual hero is Boriska. The film aims to show an infectious, frenzied energy emerging from such a troubled epoch: it awakens in Boriska and bursts into flame with the bell.'

5 · *Solaris*

Andrey Rublyov had still not been released when, in October 1968, Tarkovsky approached the studio with a project to film *Solaris*, a novel by the well-known Polish science-fiction writer Stanislaw Lem.[1]

For those who already knew and loved Tarkovsky's work, it seemed a strange choice; traditionally, science fiction was very much a popular genre, seeming to have no point of contact with Tarkovsky's style.

Of course, it is true that Lem is one of the more serious writers within this genre, but however philosophical his work the events described in the novel are absorbing in a way reminiscent of yet another often-despised genre: the horror story.

Scientists on a space station have long been engaged in fruitless attempts to make contact with the mysterious planet of Solaris and the Ocean that enfolds it. They are joined by a newcomer, a psychologist called Chris Kelvin, whose brief is to make sense of the strange happenings reported from the station and to close it down together with all the fruitless experiments taking place within it. At first he thinks that the few scientists remaining on the station have all gone mad. Then he himself becomes the victim of a harrowing delusion: he is visited by Hari, the woman he once loved and who committed suicide long ago. He tries to destroy the 'ghost', but Hari returns again and again. It gradually becomes clear that the ghosts who visit the station are simulacra made not of ordinary matter but of neutrinos which are modelled by the thinking Ocean out of the human subconscious. They are a physical embodiment of all the temptations, desires and suppressed guilt that torment the human mind.

Lem has no interest in the usual science-fiction 'war of the worlds'; the problem of *Solaris* is that of contact with a gigantic, conscious and reasoning organism: the Ocean. 'It is the Unknown which awaits us amongst the stars' is the phrase with which the author summed up the theme of this novel, written on the threshold of the space age.

Of course, even the most detailed novel creates a wide and varied range of possibilities for a film-maker. Quite apart from the option of a futuristic suspense thriller in the Hitchcock vein, the sixties had already produced such sophisticated philosophical variations on traditional science-fiction themes as Godard's *Alphaville* and Kubrick's *2001: A Space Odyssey*.

When, ten years after Lem's novel was first published, Tarkovsky conceived the idea of putting it on the screen, he innocently wrote in his application: 'Audiences are eager for a good science-fiction film, and it is common knowledge that there is great interest in the idea of one being produced here for the domestic market. The plot of *Solaris* is taut and sharp, full of unexpected twists and turns and exciting confrontations . . . We can be sure from the start that the film will be a financial success.' There is no reason to suspect him of being disingenuous. On the contrary, we can easily imagine that after his tribulations with *Andrey Rublyov*, where the obstacle seemed to be an apparently difficult cinematic language, the director had decided this time that he must bend over backwards to meet the audience's expectations. He knew as well as anyone that a film without an audience, however good it might look on the screen, has not come to life: it is the audience that brings it into being.

One wonders whether Tarkovsky already realized that if he turned to a popular, mass form (and to one of the very best novels written in that form), he would find there not a plot with unexpected twists and turns, or a magical box of surprises, but something quite different: a 'never-never land' where a chance remark, a snatch of discussion at table or a passing glance at some everyday object could acquire an existential meaning. Whatever Tarkovsky had in mind, Lem was paid for the screen rights, and once again the arguments began between the author of the novel and the author of the future film.

At the outset, as in *Ivan's Childhood*, Tarkovsky decided to make one important change in the story: in this case, it concerned the setting for the action. In the novel, everything takes place on the space station, while in the screenplay there is a prelude set on Earth.

In fact the first draft of the script did contain a relatively important distortion of the original idea: the introduction of a new and important character, Chris's wife, Maria. Chris's meeting with Hari on the station is a means of gaining knowledge of himself and cleansing his soul. This early version ends with him returning to Maria on earth, his guilt forgiven and exculpated.

Lem wrote to the director, complaining that the screen adaptation 'supplanted the tragic conflict inherent in progress with a cyclical, biological idea . . . not to mention the way it reduced the ethical and philosophical conflicts involved to nothing more than the melodrama of a family squabble'. Tarkovsky did not argue. Perhaps he also was already aware that too much excess in the plot was not a good idea. In any case, he was eager to start. He wrote to Lem: 'Soon the studio will begin work on *Solaris*. You can't imagine, Stanislaw, how glad I am of that! At last I can get down to work.'

The character of Maria was taken out, but Tarkovsky did not want to do without the prologue on Earth. As with *Ivan's Childhood*, this desire to look beyond the plot was not just a whim, but a real need. Most directors in his place would have expanded their main effort on the space station and the thinking Ocean (and indeed a chemistry laboratory was asked to look for ways in which it could be depicted); but Tarkovsky put no less effort into his search for the most ordinary of locations for the Earth sequences.

The location for Chris Kelvin's family home was found sixty-three kilometres from Moscow, near Zvenigorod, not far from the Savvino-Storozhevsky Monastery. Tarkovsky also found a place on the river Ruza for the opening sequence of the film.

Long grass . . . autumn leaves on a slow-flowing expanse of water . . . the trail of a shell falling to the bottom of the river . . . someone's feet among enormous damp burdock leaves . . . a distant cuckoo . . . a horse clip-clopping by . . . rain pouring noisily down on to the open veranda of a stone cottage. If the fifteenth-century *Rublyov* started with a prologue of premature airborne flight, the space-age *Solaris* begins with its feet firmly on the earth.

When the film was released, science-fiction buffs were unanimous in their disapproval of this terrestrial addition. Tarkovsky was accused of having failed to understand the novel and of being wedded to his 'usual anthropocentrism'. Not that this was something he would ever renounce; for art, he felt, *was* naturally anthropocentric. What else could it be?

The essential point of the change is that he furnished Chris Kelvin with a family home, full of memories: family photographs; the whole physical texture of earthly life; the sound of the rain, the dawn chorus, the flowing depths of the river, the damp of the garden, the spreading crown of an oak, the living flame of a bonfire, the bent back of his father and the gingery-grey on his temples – everything, in short, which we normally take for granted until the loss of it haunts us.[2] It could be said that nothing happens in the scenes on Earth. All that happens is life itself.

Ivan's Childhood begins before the story proper – in the freedom of dreams, in an idyll lit by the summer sun. Likewise, *Andrey Rublyov* ends after the story proper, in the calm light of the Trinity. These lyrical digressions are all the more important because the lives shown within the films they frame can boast no such sustained periods of peace.

Perhaps it should be noted here that what used to be called an 'experience' has now become a 'trauma'; what used to be 'qualms of conscience' have now become 'stress'. This is not because words are getting shorter or people are changing. Something has changed in our relationship with our environment. Man is also a part of the ecological problem.

In Tarkovsky's films his heroes strive through trauma and stress, not towards that peace that comes with experience of life, but towards an ideal harmony, like that of which the twelve-year-old Ivan dreams in the war, and to which Andrey Rublyov penetrates in the harmony of his Trinity.

The proposal Tarkovsky submitted to the studio stated that he was particularly concerned with the 'ideal of moral purity to which our descendants must remain true in order to prevail on the way to perfection of reason, honour and morality . . . In order to create the future, we need a clear conscience and honourable intentions.'

Of course, in Lem's novel we also find, alongside the intellectual problem of the encounter with the unknown, an all too human side typical of the early sixties when the novel was written. This can be summed up in a word that was fashionable at the time: 'non-communication'. Humans cannot make contact with the Ocean. But the men on the orbital station are not only separated by a lack of understanding from the planet Solaris, they are also fatally alienated from one another by their shameful thoughts and secret sins. His old love, who died on Earth and is returned to Chris Kelvin by a strange trick of nature, turns out to be cut from a different cloth, made of a different kind of matter, neutrino-matter. This is the materialization of a metaphor that in many works of the sixties expressed a psychological conflict of some kind.

However, this had not previously been a concern of Tarkovsky. If the author of the novel chose Chris Kelvin as the hero and focal point of the story, the author of the film chooses Hari for that role, without particularly going out of his way to stress the fact. It is she who strives to understand Chris, to complete her 'earthly experience' by understanding man with the aid of an external viewpoint – the viewpoint of space. She materializes (at first, just as a shell) on the abandoned but still inhabited station; she is no more and no less humanised than its inhabitants, and we are graphically reminded of how limited their lives are by the rustle of strips of paper on the station, reminding the space scientists of the rustling of leaves in the same distant way that a page of shorthand reminds us of living speech.

In the work of Tarkovsky the life of the human spirit always flows within the banks of nature and the arts; in the film the station is filled with memories of Earth, with the fruits of its culture as well as the perfect mechanisms that are the fruits of its technology. For this reason the 'space' aspect of the film's design is not of paramount importance. In fact, Tarkovsky did not make any special effort to imagine what the men of the future would be like; it is enough for him that they are human beings, recognizable as such to us, the viewers. The same can be said of their environment.

The one quality which unites everything on the orbital station, from the hi-tech white furniture, through the silver fabric of the overalls, to the consoles, gauges and rockets is their 'used' look – as used as everything looked in the monastery yard in the early 1400s.

To be fair to Tarkovsky, in the scene where Hari, locked in the cabin by Chris, bursts through the metal door and falls senseless to the ground; when she tries to commit suicide by drinking liquid oxygen and then comes painfully and relentlessly back to life; and in the atmosphere of desolation and terror on the station – in all these he showed himself in perfect command of the techniques of the horror film. He discovered their secret in exactly the same way as he discovered the secret of making historical films: completely faithful, naturalistic authenticity – only this time the authenticity of the unreal. The main thing for him, however, was something else: the way in which Hari, finding herself at the centre of the clashes of personality and point of view on the station, having started as a ghost, gradually becomes a human being.

One cannot be a human being without knowing 'love for the graves of our ancestors'. In spite of being born out of nothing, she comes to know, together with Chris, the strange and detailed world of the 'Winter Morning' which Brueghel's picture spreads over the convex surface of the earth. A short piece of film from Earth preserves something both intimate and unrepeatable, but which belongs to the whole of humanity. This is the poets' 'bonfire smoke', the 'bending image of the mother', and the 'sky – a book like any other' of which Aleksandr Blok wrote.

But this, the 'saving bitterness of homesickness', is not enough. Hari also learns the difficult business of conscience.

Tarkovsky's Chris Kelvin leaves to Sartorius the hackneyed role of pure scientist and himself makes the only constructive contribution to the earthmen's work on Solaris: he allows his feelings of guilt, conscience and love to be awakened. He puts all that is most human in him at the disposal of science, and agrees to an experiment whereby his inner world is projected down on to the Ocean.

When he awakens, Hari is no longer on the station. She has disappeared again, this time for ever, voluntarily submitting herself to annihilation. By sacrificing herself, she has achieved human stature.

The Ocean has responded to that most personal signal, the heart's memory, to the bitterness of Chris Kelvin's nostalgia in which the figures of the woman who bore him and the woman he loved, his guilt and expiation, his own house and his own Earth with its sounds and smells and the rain pouring down on to the open veranda, all have their own appointed place.[3] Except . . . the rain is falling indoors, and Chris is standing outside, in the garden, looking through the window at his father who does not notice the water pouring down his shoulders. It is the image of a familiar yet strange looking-glass world, called into being out of nothingness by the living and mysterious Ocean of Solaris.

So the film ends. Is this the contact for which they were hoping? Or is it another of those images of the artist, achieving harmony by what Pasternak called the 'effort of resurrection'?

The film was released on 20 March 1972 and, as though to compensate for the tribulations of *Andrey Rublyov*, was immediately offered to the Cannes Film Festival.

Over the decade that had passed since Tarkovsky first burst upon the world in Venice, the prestige of film festivals had become somewhat tarnished in the artistic world. No longer did anyone expect the stunning revelations of former years, and if the prize-winning films of the early sixties had passed straight from festival screens into history, the prizes now tended to go to films that were merely well made, witty and topical.

Solaris did not repeat the sensation of *Andrey Rublyov*, but it was treated with respect. After Kubrick's *2001: A Space Odyssey*, with which Tarkovsky was in open disagreement, the set of the orbital station seemed to lack effect. The rhythms of the film were too measured for a thriller or a horror film; to some it seemed simply boring. But even if Tarkovsky was not hailed as the author of a cinema sensation, his status as a major artist, a moralist and a humanist was confirmed.

From some quarters, however, he was accused of being overattached to violence. The point is worth considering. Physical pain seems to us to be a gross imperfection, a stupid mistake of nature. But when medicine finds a way of killing pain, it is sometimes depriving us of an important early warning system. We need pain for self-preservation. This is why Tarkovsky's Chris Kelvin, unlike Sartorius, with his courage of all-embracing reason, displays the courage of feeling and learns anew how to suffer.

In the art of our country and time there have been many heroes who have had the courage to overcome suffering, but fewer who have had the courage to suffer for their guilt and that of others in the tradition of Russian literature. Without these martyrs of conscience, humanity risks being deprived of a similar kind of early warning system.

And if we leave aside our legitimate anthropocentrism and imagine for a moment, as in the novel, that life on our small Earth is just a chance event – one of the by-products of the method of trial and error practised by an indifferent universe – what would the universe see in the sum total of our joys and sufferings, our mistakes and successes that might be worth preserving? Would it not be that little ache in the heart that we call conscience, which stands guard over our reason, capable in its hubris of destroying its own self by mistake? Is it not for this one thing, as Dostoevsky liked to say, that the cosmos needs humanity?

Tarkovsky on *Solaris*

'Whether my first two films were good or bad, they were really about the same thing: fidelity at whatever the cost to a moral duty, the struggle to fulfil that duty, belief in what has to be done even at the expense of personal conflicts, the force of convictions, all in a character with a highly individual destiny, where disaster can strike without breaking the human spirit.

'Both Ivan and Andrey have total disregard for their safety. Ivan in the physical sense, Andrey in the moral sense. In their actions they are seeking a moral ideal.'

'As far as Stanislaw Lem's *Solaris* is concerned, my decision to film it does not denote any affection for the science-fiction genre. For me, the important thing is that *Solaris* poses a problem that means a lot to me: the problem of striving and achieving through your convictions; of moral transformation in the struggle in one man's life. The profound thought behind Lem's novel has nothing to do with the science-fiction genre in which it is written, and a love of science fiction would not be enough to make you like the film.'

'For some reason in all the science-fiction films which I have ever seen, the audience is forced into a detailed, close-up examination of what the future will look like. Indeed, often (like Stanley Kubrick) they call their films "visions of the future" . . . I would like to film *Solaris* in such a way that the audiences are not faced with something technologically outlandish.

'If, for instance, we were to film passengers getting into a tram as something never before seen or even heard of, then it would look like Kubrick's moon-landing sequence. But if we film a moon-landing the way they film a tram-stop in an ordinary film, then everything will be as we would wish it.'

'I have noticed from my own work that if the external, emotional structure of images in the film is built on the author's own memories, on a link between his own life and the fabric of the film, then the audience will feel the emotional effect. If, on the other hand, the director follows only the external, literary line (whether he be working from a work of literature or a specially written film-script), however much care he puts into his work, the audience will remain cold.

'So if you are not capable of affecting the audience as the great writers do by building on its own experience, then in the cinema what you should do is build on your own.'

6 · *Mirror*

The table, same for great-grandsire and grandson . . .

Arseniy Tarkovsky

Mirror marked the fullest expression of Tarkovsky's personality as director. It also had the most convoluted history of any of his films.

In principle Tarkovsky was against experimentation in film production. Nonetheless, his work on this script amounted to one long experiment, intended to create a film in the way that a work of literature is created. Tarkovsky had always been inspired by the idea of the cinema as equal to the other arts from the point of view of authorship, and *Mirror* was to be his fullest expression of this idea.

The first version was almost entirely devoted to his mother. 'I cannot reconcile myself to the thought that my mother will ever die. I will protest and shout that she is immortal. I want to convince others of her individuality and uniqueness. The internal premise from which I started was my desire to analyse her character in such a way as to prove her immortality.' It would be hard to imagine a plan more difficult to implement – not only practically but ethically – than the one Tarkovsky proposed to the studio under the original title of *Confession* in 1968, the same year as *Solaris*.

The script (which Tarkovsky continued to work on until shooting started) was quite clearly influenced by television – which had already started to affect the cinema very strongly. Tarkovsky offered the studio a 'questionnaire-film', developed from the familiar television genre, but which he would justify by its artistic content.[1] He proposed that the film would consist of three strata of material. The fundamental one would be an interview putting the widest possible range of questions to his own mother, Maria Ivanovna Vishnyakova. These would touch on all kinds of subjects: her attitude to space exploration; what she thought of the Vietnam war; did she or did she not believe in God; as well as more personal questions about her family and about her inner life. As proposed, it would have been like a session with a psychoanalyst, where you are asked to remember your most shameful actions and your most tragic or happy experiences. She would be asked about her love for her husband and for her children. At the same time it would be a filmed interview on matters of general interest. The list of questions included in the script was endless.

Another stratum was to be provided by 'facts' from the past, i.e. acted sequences of reminiscence from the author's own childhood. The third strand would be newsreels, and it was from a combination of these last two that the film would eventually be made. The initial plan, however, required a female psychiatrist, pretending to help in the task of collecting material for the script, to interview his mother, in her own flat, without the mother being aware of what was going on, thanks to the use of three hidden cameras.[2]

But what is the ethical position of a director who intends to provoke his own mother to speak frankly in a way that she never would in front of a camera, and then make public all that she has said? A confession expressed for all one's fellow men is a genre that has been a tradition since the days of Jean-Jacques Rousseau. However, we have not yet reached the stage when we can force someone else into such a confession. And that is why the questionnaire, which survived for a long time in the versions of the script, did not in fact continue beyond the paper stage.

A point arrived where the file was closed on *Confession* since Tarkovsky started shooting *Solaris*. It would not be opened again until 1973, now known as *Bright, Bright Day*. The 'mother' and 'childhood' stories were more fully explored in this version than they would be in the final one, and there was no Natalia or Ignat; in other words, no hint yet of the past being echoed by 'doubles' in the present.

This script opens with a 'bright, bright' winter's day at the cemetery. A funeral is in progress: death meeting the hero, as Pasternak put it, 'like an official land-surveyor', measuring the grave.

'Death completes the final *montage* of our lives,' wrote Pier Paolo Pasolini, 'and after death, when the stream of our life is finished, the meaning of that stream can emerge.'[3]

From this vantage-point – the bright, bright day at the cemetery – the lyrical hero of the film looks back into the magical world of his childhood memories.

... The boy stands with his French governess in a crowd of people watching the demolition of a derelict village church in 1939.[4]

... The mother runs through the rain to the printing works because she thinks that a mistake has crept into a very important edition.

... During the war, the mother sells little bunches of flowers at the market, and the son helps her in the thankless task of picking the ugly, skimpy little bouquets.

... As the mother is coming home with the children through the forest paths at night, they are filled with an irrational (though perfectly understandable) fear.

... A shell-shocked cadet instructor who is laughed at by his pupils saves them by throwing himself on to a hand grenade.

... The mother, now a grandmother, goes to look after her grandson at his riding lesson and the son remembers a horse bolting and nearly killing him.

All these sequences, most of them concerning the mother, go to make up the proud and pathetic picture of an abandoned woman who in the son's mind is associated with Dostoevsky's 'oppressed and humiliated'.

Half these sequences, such as the demolition of the church, the flower-selling, the forest at night and the riding lesson, fell by the wayside, while others, like the printing works, selling the ear-rings,[5] the cadet instructor, grew, changed and coalesced if not into a real 'plot', then into a series of free associations that was joined by a new and equally important theme: the hero's relationship with his wife and the way in which the tangled skein of their quarrels is almost a mirror-image of the break-up of the marriage of his parents.

The doubling of the mother and the wife, just like the 'mirror' theme in *Solaris*, seems to have been ready and waiting to be adopted here. Many interpretations can be given to the title Tarkovsky finally chose to give to the film, but perhaps not the least important of these is the idea expressed by the drunken Snaut in *Solaris*; what humanity needs is not the Cosmos, but a mirror for himself: 'What Man needs is Man'.

Man may need Man, but in the meantime:

How can the heart express itself?
How can another understand?
How can he know what moves your soul?[6]

The film eventually started at a point after the break between the father and mother has already taken place; it only remained for the implications of this separation to become a part of everyday life for the family.

The film actually opens with a prologue: the treatment for stuttering was filmed from life, and it remains as a rudimentary vestige of the 'television' idea in the original script. The prologue is a kind of paraphrase of the confession theme, stated, in the broadest possible terms, as the striving towards liberation from wordlessness, the effort to break into speech. The film is full of such vestiges of discarded material, a clear indication of what the psychologists call 'substitution'. In spite of everything, however, the prologue does remain on the level of that allegory which the director always claimed to dislike so much.

The poetry of the film is introduced after the prologue, with a leaning wattle fence, and the mother looking out along a forest path that stretches away into the darkness among the trees.

The episode with the chance passer-by who suddenly appears round the bend in the path is loaded with emotional significance: he is not the father, the one who has left the family and will never come back again. The character seems to have been introduced to allow Tarkovsky to include in the film his favourite actor, Solonitsyn, who had already played the title role in *Andrey Rublyov* and the memorable Sartorius in *Solaris*. This strange man with his high-domed forehead seems to trail an envelope of resonant vitality and the richness of some unrevealed future potential. But there is no hope for his character here: the young woman has already made her choice, the zealously self-sacrificing one of bringing up her children alone.

Like Fellini, Tarkovsky could have called his film 'Amarcord' ('I Remember'). Laying aside the funeral, and substituting the hero's crisis in the finale, he still retains his own presence in the film. His 'remembering' takes place in the most literal way, as an off-screen monologue brought to life visually by the images on the screen.

For my generation, the film also holds the elusive charm of recognition; since we share so many of the protagonist's childhood memories, it could just as well have been called 'We Remember'. Those dark hallways in the wooden village houses that smelled of resin, dust and paraffin; the lace curtains blowing in the wind; the narrow glass chimney of the table-lamp; the mica window in the paraffin heater and the smoky little flame inside; those glass jars, illogically copying the shape of the traditional earthenware pot, that people used to fill with bunches of wild flowers; the pot itself, with fresh milk cool from the cellar, huge cold drops of condensation on the outside; and the mother's dress, embroidered linen, the sort you could buy for coupons; her hair, knotted carelessly on the tender nape of her neck – this semi-urban, semi-rural existence led by those with a little house in the woods outside Moscow or another city, the fragile pre-war days of our childhood, are conveyed in Rerberg's camerawork with a rare and almost magical solidity.

> If to the fleeting hour I say
> Remain! . . .

Might not Mephistopheles have been anticipating the cinema, when he made his bargain with Faust? It would seem to be the case for Tarkovsky. He savours the gust of wind that blows over the lamp, sweeping from the table its narrow glass chimney and a heavy loaf of black bread, while making the tree-tops boil; then he comes back to it, slows it down, draws it out, and relishes this 'hour so sweet' of childhood's oneness with the world, as a sculptor relishes the clay with pleasure. Nowhere else would this kind of 'fact' – the cinema as 'imprinted time' – be embodied as fully in his work as in *Mirror*.

His desire to show the facts led to the disintegration of his narrative structure, which in turn led (perhaps even against the author's original intentions) to an abundance of all kinds of rhetorical devices –

metonymy, ellipse, simile, aposiopesis and other, purely cinematic figures – all of which demand an effort of interpretation from the audience. *Mirror* is the most concrete, but also the most indirect of Tarkovsky's films; the most documentary, while also the most poetic.

Also documentary are the poems of Arseniy Tarkovsky, Andrey's father, which are read by the poet himself. The actual presence on the screen of his old mother is equally documentary. But this immediately necessitates a 'double exposure' of the character, when one and the same person appears in two separate manifestations, or two different people are the same character at different times. Ignat, for instance, is both himself and the author when he was a child.

Tarkovsky set his leading actress a challenging task: to play the same kind of character at two different periods – as a pre-war woman and as the post-war 'emancipated' type. Margarita Terekhova magnificently succeeds in the task. She re-creates both the old-fashioned, delicate but tough femininity of our mothers, and the bravado of the woman of today whose self-sufficiency and freedom are the other side of loneliness.

'Love' themes as such have never particularly interested Tarkovsky, except as a part of some wider issue. In *Mirror* we pass through the generations to see that love is always fragile, and always likely to leave a woman alone in life, with children to bring up and a bond of love for them that will also let her down when the children grow up and she grows old. Each generation, while undergoing its own experience, is brought face to face with the same accursed and eternal questions, while the chain of love and motherhood stretches back beyond the remotest infinity.

A double and triple exposure of the character thus takes on the significance of an almost mythological coupling of similarity and distinction. (It is not for nothing, for instance, that the hero answers 'Yes' the first time and 'No' the second when Natalia asks if she is like his mother.) These complex relationships and the play of time substitute for a narrative thread in the film.

The film would undoubtedly have been 'easier' if it had been constructed in the familiar manner of the family narrative, where the history of an era is revealed through the experience of one family. Such an approach is pushed to the limit in the printing-press episode, where the psychological atmosphere of the Stalin era and the 'cult of personality' are conveyed through the story of a small (in the end, it turns out, non-existent) misprint.[7]

The unusual quality of *Mirror* lies in its juxtaposition of time scales that are normally subject to different yardsticks of measurement. Two people, both wounded by the war, the instructor and the schoolboy cadet, are waging their own small war on the school firing-range. This sequence is cut into a newsreel of soldiers, dragging their weapons through the endless mud of their war-torn land, pulling on and on through the mud, through rivers, through the years of the war, to the distant final victory. History enters the microcosm of remembered events, without being reduced to a part of the plot. Its time flows in a different way from the micro-span of the human pulse. The boy stands on a hill, a bird flies down towards him – suddenly we hear the victory celebrations and see Hitler's corpse beside the Wolf's Lair. Here, in effect, the space in the frame broadens to the universal point of view in Brueghel's pictures, while the music of Bach and Purcell gives an elegiac gravity to the grey, muddy pictures of the newsreel.

Indeed, art and the newsreel were the two points of reference which defined the world of Tarkovsky's films from *Ivan's Childhood* onwards. In *Mirror*, art enters Aleksei's life with a fat pre-revolutionary volume on Leonardo da Vinci which lies on the table in the house in the forest. Art takes its hold on his impressionable soul, and transforms the world of memories so that Solovyova, the doctor's wife, and all the comfortable, well-fed details of the life she leads in spite of the war, including her cherubic baby swathed in lace, unexpectedly assume the colours and textures of the High Renaissance.

Into this sequence is cut another newsreel, of the first air-ships. The age of flying balloons and Zeppelins is as much a part of our childhood as the news from the front in Spain, the first bombings of Madrid and Spanish children being sent away to safety.

The theme of the Motherland, paradoxically, is introduced through the strange, musical rhythms of the Spanish language. Why Spanish? Because those Spanish refugees – no longer children, but still retaining their Spanish identity – still live in our country. Again, history and ordinary lives coexist, side by side, never pretending to fit neatly one into the other, but remaining a complex of dialectical contradictions.

That is why there are no answers to the questions posed in this film: Why did the hero's father leave his family? Why does Aleksei's and Natalia's marriage not last?

There are no answers, and therein lies the guilt. That is why Aleksei peers, as in a mirror, into the impenetrability of his parents' relations – because first love, comprehensible or incomprehensible, is all we will ever see when we look. The irrelevant litany of mutual hurts and resentments that Natalia and he recite to each other does not absolve their guilt, or calm their conscience, or quench the thirst for absolute love that is as insistent as our need for ideal harmony.

Likewise, the film expresses the theme of motherhood, through this mother, with her difficult personality and her hard life, both of which are fated to be repeated over and over again, as in a series of mirrors, however simple it might seem to admit mistakes and learn from experience. Remember the scene where the mother, still young, stares long and hard into a clouded mirror until there, in its depths, is revealed another face, her own when old? 'From the other side of the mirror's glass', wrote Arseniy Tarkovsky. Science fiction would call it a time machine. But it is merely memory, which substitutes for the fourth dimension in our normal three-dimensional world and allows time to flow in any direction as it never does in reality. This special awareness of space–time relationships is particularly highly developed in Tarkovsky.

The director takes us through different aspects of memory – memory as conscience and memory as guilt – and then combines within the space of one final sequence two points in time, or three if we take into account the montage structure: There is the young woman, still only expecting her first child, who sees the field and the path leading off into the distance; there is the old woman she sees – leading by the hand those same three close-cropped children in the baggy shirts of the pre-war age; and as a young woman again, but now abandoned at the other end of the field ('Living your life is not a field to be crossed!'), looking forward into the future that has yet to come about.

With this idealized image of a mother's love, changeless in time, set in a strange space which combines two different times in one frame, the director ends his journey, one which encompasses all the memorable crossroads of Soviet life. This complex film is human and ultimately simple in its motifs: history, art, homeland and home.

The final version of the script was delivered in the middle of 1973; shooting began in September of that year and was finished by March 1974. Then began the editing, which was a harder task than for any of the previous films. The crew could hardly believe it when at last the film was ready.

Compared with *Andrey Rublyov*, the incubation period for *Mirror* was relatively compressed, but eventful. The stumbling block was, as before, the old argument about the film's accessibility. Tarkovsky formulated his position at one of the preliminary Mosfilm discussions:

> Since the cinema is, after all, an art, then it cannot be expected to be 'easy to understand'. Nobody demands that of the other arts . . . I see no point at all in mass-appeal . . .
>
> A myth has come into being that I am inaccessible and incomprehensible. It would be impossible to establish oneself as an individual with anything to contribute without differentiating the audience.

This 'differentiating the audience' which was the usual result of the films produced by Tarkovsky was never so polarized as with *Mirror*. I well remember the first showing at the Union of Cinematographers, because I was used as a battering-ram by someone who broke a plate-glass door to get in. Everyone wanted to see the film. Tarkovsky himself said that none of his other films met with such a wide spread of reactions from his fellow film-makers, some affronted, others delighted.

Perhaps it is the openness, the un-Russian nakedness of his personal confession that is at fault. It is not at all in the tradition of our cinema.

His colleagues' reaction was such a sensitive matter for Tarkovsky that he almost decided to give up the cinema. Strangely enough, the director, so often accused of élitism, received more letters from ordinary members of the public after the release of this film than after any other. The letters were of all different kinds: some irritated, some delighted, some critical, but perhaps for the first time in his life they gave him a real sense of a human response, that response for which this shy, self-contained artist had always longed. From his own experience he was only too well aware of how little a film is worth if it does not win an audience.

Tarkovsky on *Mirror*

'*Mirror* was extremely difficult to edit: we had more than twenty different versions in the cutting-room at one time. By "different versions" I do not mean differences in a splice here or there, but different structures, a different order for the episodes. The film was not holding together, it would not stand up on its two feet, it simply fell apart; there was no sense of wholeness, no internal cohesion, no solid logic. Then, suddenly, we decided, in desperation, to rearrange it one last time, and the film took shape before our eyes.

'It took me a long time to believe that the miracle had taken place.'

'There are only about two hundred sequences in *Mirror*. This is very little, considering that in a film of this length there are usually around five hundred. The reason for the small number of sequences in *Mirror* is their actual length.'

'When the cinema escapes from the power of money (I mean production costs), when they invent a way for the author of a work of art to capture reality with his own hands (paper and pen, canvas and paint, marble and chisel, "x" and the film-maker), then we shall see. Then film will become first among the arts, and its muse the queen of all the muses.'

'When my father saw it, he said to my mother: "See what short shrift he had given us?" He said it with a smile, but there must have been something that hurt. They did not notice what short shrift I gave myself – only how I treated them.'

Part II

7 · Andrey Tarkovsky's Motifs

Perhaps before the lips, the whisper had existed,
And leaves were whirling long before the trees,
And those to whom we dedicate experience,
Were long before already formed by then.

Osip Mandelstam[1]

For those who wish to view the cinema as a purposeful, unfolding story, the comparatively few films which Andrey Tarkovsky had made up to this point did not amount to an impressive, organically developing *œuvre*. What consistency was there among two adaptations of already published books and two films based on original scripts: one vaguely contemporary and one in a remote historical setting, a venture into futuristic science fiction and a contribution to the burgeoning Soviet war genre? Meditations on the life of the artist and a highly personal confession. Strange as it may now seem, the links between these apparently diverse projects were by no means apparent to many, especially among Soviet critics of the late seventies.

It was easier indeed to see the links between Tarkovsky's stylistic quest and tendencies in world cinema during the sixties and seventies. Parallels could be found for the liberation of the camera in *The Steamroller and the Violin*, the elliptical expression of *Ivan's Childhood*, the scrupulous historical authenticity of *Andrey Rublyov* and the extreme subjectivity, equivalent to an interior monologue, of *Mirror*. Soviet film-makers, after all, had been as influenced as any by the 'fresco' structure of Fellini's *La Dolce Vita* and by the confessional intimacy of his *8½*, by the revival of expressionist techniques in Bergman's *Wild Strawberries* and by the austere asceticism of Bresson.

This was not to decry the originality of Tarkovsky's work: his name was already held in high esteeem internationally, but every artist is to some extent part and parcel of the spirit of his age. What linked him with these other great names, however, was not some similarity of method or genre, but the scale of his personality, the integral quality of his approach, always significant, even in its weaknesses.

Like every film-maker who has not only to chart his own course, but also deal with the myriad practical production aspects of his work, Tarkovsky planned from film to film, which meant that he could not constantly be concerned with the harmony of his work as a whole. Looking back, of course, he could discern a continuity of themes within it. But also, more important even than any thematic unity, there began to be apparent a number of characteristic Tarkovsky 'motifs', which recurred in film after film:

. . . The film begins in a calm idyllic setting, bathed in the summer sunlight; far off, a cuckoo is calling, while a butterfly hovers over a tow-headed boy, the huge liquid eyes of a little goat shine from the screen, the boy's mother smiles her gentle, maternal smile . . .

Tarkovsky's motifs are most in evidence when he is working on literary subject matter. Bogomolov's *Ivan* could have been filmed without the dreams, or Lem's *Solaris* without the terrestrial additions, but they would have been completely different films.

In retrospect, it now seems astonishing that when, at the beginning of his career, the young director was given a screenplay already heavily 'in debt', the very first version of *his* own *Ivan's Childhood* that he proposed to the studio already contained the dream sequences almost exactly as they were finally to appear on the screen. All their vivid dream logic and conviction were already there in that first draft, including the cuckoo's summer call, the falling rain, the long-necked horses thoughtfully chewing the apples on the white sand, the girl, and even the black tree that rounds off the last sequence like an exclamation mark, a warning of danger. It is as though these images were not invented especially for the occasion by Tarkovsky, but were something which had always existed – before the film; before the written page – for him to plunge the war-scorched iron of Bogomolov's prose into the depths of their limpid peace.

Now, almost twenty years later, leafing through the material in the archives I was again surprised to confirm that those dream sequences were not youthful improvisations with a camera, but solidly-constructed edifices, conceived in advance of their transfer to paper or to film – and thus tangible witness to the spiritual world of the director himself. And this is why Tarkovsky, however often he turned to literature for the subject matter of his films, would always remain the *author* of what he produced. If the writer of the work he had chosen was also a strong-minded individual, conflict was bound to arise, not because Tarkovsky was too free with his material, but simply because there was no other way in which he could work.

. . . The white stone wall of a church; against it, the patchy body of an air-balloon, sewn together from different-coloured sheepskins and pieces of leather, looks even uglier. There is a hum of voices and an astonished, joyful cry: 'I'm flying!' The whole earth with its churches, rivers and herds unfolds, then spins like a globe beneath the feet of this antediluvian air-traveller . . .

There is, however, one visual motif in the original notes for Ivan's dreams which never reached the screen: the film was intended to start with Ivan flying through the trees. The director intended to add this sequence by means of superimposition, and came back to the idea frequently at various stages of the shooting. Why did the idea remain only on paper? Perhaps the technical problems were too great; perhaps the idea of superimposition seemed too old-fashioned; perhaps the idea in itself seemed too far fetched? It survived, however, in a hidden sense, for the film begins with a flight by the camera, as it accompanies Ivan's headlong rush downhill. Interestingly, the motif of flight, once established, would recur in subsequent films, with as little external motivation.

In *Andrey Rublyov* it is embodied with the same tangible authenticity that characterizes the whole of this film. While the film was still at the script stage its tenuous links with the sketchily known life-story of the real Rublyov were severed, and once the biographical purpose fell away, what was left was the vivid image of the 'flying peasant'.[2]

In the script it originally figured as 'winged flight'. During the shooting (this is one of those cases where Tarkovsky did change his original vision) a different method was decided upon:

We spent a long time looking for a way to break down the visual symbolism on which this episode was based, and eventually decided that the wings were the problem. In order to eliminate comparisons with Icarus, we invented the balloon. It would be clumsy, strung together from skins, ropes and pieces of cloth. I consider that it did away with the false romance of the sequence, and gave it a fresh and unique quality.[3]

However, neither the elimination of the 'false romance', nor the tangible, concrete quality of the event could rob this prologue of its emotional power as an image of man's potential, and of his spiritual striving to go beyond the ordinary bounds of his life on earth. It is this meaning that gives the prologue its place in the film. This is another case where that term so hated by Tarkovsky, 'metaphor', is apt – not least because the rest of the film is an embodiment, on various planes, of that spiritual striving and its victory over the obduracy of matter.

This dislike of the term 'metaphor' is understandable; it springs partly from the hackneyed use of 'heroic' metaphor in Stalinist cinema; and partly from his wish to avoid the rhetoric of allegory. Thus, for him, the flight motif represented a deeper and more vital symbol than something merely allegorical.

Air travel has long since become an everyday reality, but it was obviously not its mechanical aspect which most concerned Tarkovsky. In *Solaris* Chris Kelvin's family home is full of old engravings of hot-air balloons, in spite of Kelvin's space-age profession. And during the technical planning for *Solaris*, one of the most important special effects for Tarkovsky was weightlessness, for he insisted on Chris and Hari being able to float gently beneath the ceiling of their interplanetary cabin.

In *Mirror*, too, the mother and father float – this time without any scientific 'justification'; this sequence was particularly distasteful to the film's critics.

Why? Can it be that the feeling of nausea which almost overcomes the young woman, compounded of hunger, disgust and shame when the doctor's wife asks her to kill a chicken, is less of a justification than the technical term, 'weightlessness'? 'What a pity that I only ever think of you at bad moments like this' is what the mother is thinking, addressing in her mind the husband who left her so long ago. It is the 'bad moment' that lifts them above the purely material world, just as Chris and Hari are lifted by a 'good moment' far more surely than by mere freedom from the laws of gravity. Nobody, after all, demands narrative justification for all the flying done by lovers in the pictures of Marc Chagall.

Mirror, too, contains a passing reference to vintage balloon travel. When choosing newsreel films to include, Tarkovsky did not take the famous Polar flights; he chose, instead, some very uneventful footage of a Zeppelin being checked before a flight, either because the enormous balloon reduces the human figures to such insignificant size, or because the natural silence of the subject went well with the music of Purcell; or, again, perhaps because we remember the tragic fate of the crew. Whatever the reason, the image was chosen not on account of some logical link, but because of the gravity and resonance which it brings to the film.[4]

'Why don't people fly?' asks the unsophisticated heroine of Ostrovsky's nineteenth-century play *The Storm*. We must not make too much of this motif in Tarkovsky's work, or indeed of any other motif. But in an age where man has learned by mechanical means to fly faster than the speed of sound, where our physical nature has been far outstripped by our technological achievements, there is an especially poignant ring to the unsophisticated question: 'Why don't people fly?'

. . . *So* Ivan's Childhood *began before the story proper, in the freedom of dreams, in an idyll lit by the summer sun. And so* Andrey Rublyov *ended after the story proper, in the calm light of the* Trinity.

However closely a film follows the book upon which it is based, there is always something left for the camera to say that the written word could never have expressed: the physical existence of the images portrayed. The cinema can give solid reality to a literary image. In *Ivan's Childhood* instead of building a set for the battalion field station, Tarkovsky found a derelict church. It has become almost one of the traditions of the cinema today to have something happen in a derelict church. The vaulted crypt, where Ivan climbs up on to a beam with the little bell and sounds the alarm; the piece of wall with the remains of a provincial 'Flight into Egypt' – all this would be nothing more than a felicitous discovery on location were it not for the fact that in Tarkovsky's next film, *Andrey Rublyov*, the same visual motif has developed into the subject matter itself, with church, frescoes and bell carrying a semantic load that encompasses what Pushkin called, 'the fate of a man, the fate of a people'. Here he showed the white-stone cathedral as the work of human culture; its destruction an image of catastrophe for the nation ('snow in the cathedral').[5] The huge bell, still warm in its scaffolding and ropes, is an image of courage and rebirth; the tender ochre, blue and delicate gold of the *Trinity* signify the climax of the struggle to prevail over the troubles of this earth – an image of final harmony. The shimmering halo of meanings is wider than any mere expression of it in words could convey. At stake is not the fate of the Church itself – although in *Mirror* Tarkovsky returned to the idea of a church being demolished in 1939[6] – but of something greater, something which is holy for the whole nation. That is why Chris Kelvin takes a small reproduction of Rublyov's *Trinity* to the Solaris orbital station with him, and Gibarian, the Armenian, takes a picture of Echmiadzin, the central shrine of the Armenian church.

Tarkovsky's recurrent motifs in his first four films underwent a variety of Protean transformations. Some change as a function of what Stanislavsky calls the 'available circumstances'. Others change in volume and significance, present in one film as a hint, in another as an integral part of the plot or as a whole semantic system; later they would shrink again to an echo, a resonance, a mere flicker in the memory. In *Mirror* the hero's flat has an *Andrey Rublyov* poster on the wall. It is not simply a bridge between the author and the character, but the now familiar icon of the Trinity, symbolizing a nation's culture and traditions that are an essential part of the spiritual world of the film.

Tarkovsky's recurrent motifs were not always visual. Consider, for example, stuttering. First Ivan stuttered, then Boriska. In the script for *Mirror* the military instructor stuttered. In the actual film this motif emerged in the prologue more completely than anywhere else in Tarkovsky's work: stuttering not only as a physical handicap, but as the expression of a dumbness of the spirit, a wound to the individual's inner life. Art is revealed as the cure for this dumbness, freeing and healing the dumb, just as *Mirror* is not only a film but a confession by the artist as well.

So faithful was the director to his recurrent motifs that even if one of them was not to be found in any particular film, leafing through earlier versions of the script is sure to reveal it, at least in some latent sense, lying ready to re-emerge in the next film. Sometimes they are there as variations: Andrey Rublyov's silence, for instance, is an extreme – and deliberate – case of dumbness, cured, once again, by art.

Tarkovsky's early work is also full of much more straightforward, immediately recognizable motifs: there was the apple the little violinist placed before the girl with the ribbon in Tarkovsky's diploma film; the shop window full of mirrors . . .

Sometimes the constancy of these motifs even seems obtrusive: after the epilogue to *Rublyov* in colour, a harmony of gentle hues, another sequence in black and white of grazing horses was tacked on for good measure.

These motifs are sometimes visual, sometimes verbal, sometimes constant, sometimes changing, sometimes abstract, sometimes concrete, but taken together, they permeate the work of Tarkovsky, flowing from film to film, linking one with another and creating something that is more than just the sum of all their separate parts: Tarkovsky's own world. This world is a world of its own elemental forces, its own climate, even its own weather.

The films contain other motifs, too universal to be easily analysed, but just as fiercely personal for Tarkovsky and just as significant in his work. The elemental forces of nature are, of course, a part of physical reality and not the private province of any one director, but who could fail to recognize the sudden, splashing downpours so beloved of Tarkovsky? The heavens open on the Muscovites watching the demolition team in *The Steamroller and the Violin*; on the lorry-load of apples in Ivan's dream; in *Mirror* the mother runs from the rain; Rublyov and his fellow travellers hide from it in the old wooden hut; for Chris Kelvin it embodies all that is most dear in his dream of Earth. 'Tarkovsky's rain' is as much his own as the endless, unrelenting rain of Kurosawa. It is not only the rain, but the other elements as well: the little spark of a bonfire and the mighty flames of a conflagration; the sluggishness of a great river and the leap and play of water in a stream.

The least successful of Tarkovsky's landscapes is that of the planet Solaris and its fantastical Ocean. Evidently his imagination was less inspired by something truly from the realms of fantasy than from the real world of the Earth. On the other hand, one of the best sequences he ever filmed is the fire witnessed through the curtain of rain by the adults and children in *Mirror*, which plays no part at all in the plot. Its significance is purely as an image, as a manifestation of natural forces, an elemental spectacle that sears itself into the soul of a child, never to be forgotten.

The impressionable soul of a child, the sharpness and freshness of its perceptions, their permanence and scale in its subsequent inner life – these are clues to the single images in Tarkovsky's work which bear within them the secret of a thousand interpretations. It is this which gives complexity to the visual world of his cinema, where any motif, be it apple or mirror, can be understood and interpreted with a whole wealth of semantic and cultural detail. At the same time, it remains a solid and physical world; a world open to that natural freedom of association seen through the eyes of a child. It is the good fortune of an artist that those first impressions should still burn bright in his soul.

Tarkovsky once considered a project to film the work of Marcel Proust. Everything he had attempted in the cinema thus far had been in one way or another a 'search for time past', for the years of childhood. The dream of flight is part of the dream of early childhood and no supersonic aircraft could ever replace the sensation of flying *oneself* in that 'childish' dream.[7]

This motif of childhood reminiscences and perceptions permeated all Tarkovsky's films; it was one of the means by which he made new subject matter his own. Without plunging into the memories of Ivan or Chris Kelvin, without touching their most intimate relations with home, childhood, father and mother, he could never have made them so completely his own.

The motifs of childhood, of the loss of one or both parents, and of guilt – whatever the actual subject matter of the separate films – are the most constant aspect of Tarkovsky's work from its beginnings up to *Mirror*.

1. *Ivan's Childhood:* 'The play of fantasy and imagination'.

2. *Ivan's Childhood:* Ivan going 'over the river' on his last mission.

3. *Ivan's Childhood:* Kolya Burlyaev as Ivan with Lt. Galtsev and Captain Kholin.

4. *Andrey Rublyov:* Kolya Burlyaev as Boriska, the young bell-founder.

5. *Andrey Rublyov:* the Tartars' savage attack on Vladimir.

6. Anatoly Solonitsyn as Andrey Rublyov, the passive protagonist.

7. *Solaris:* Chris Kelvin aboard the beleaguered space station.

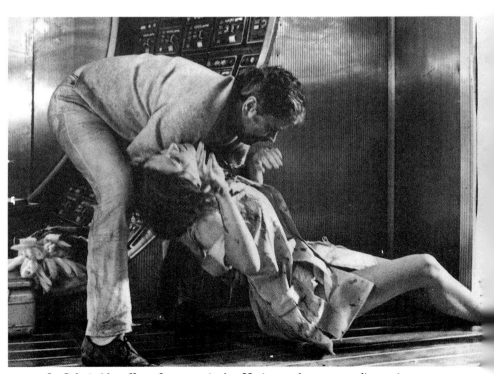

8. *Solaris:* 'the effort of resurrection' as Hari struggles to come alive again.

9. *Mirror:* Margarita Terekhova as the mother – 'proving her immortality'.

10. *Mirror:* personal history recalled through a Breughel composition.

11. Tarkovsky filming Kaidanovsky and Solonitsyn on *Stalker* (photograph courtesy of Evgeny Tsimbal).

12. *Stalker:* the trio of metaphysical adventurers enter the 'Zone'.

13. *Nostalgia*: Gorchakov's 'road to Calvary' across a muddy pool.

14. *Nostalgia*: Domenico calls upon the world to repent, before setting fire to himself on the Capitoline Hill in Rome.

15. *The Sacrifice:* Little Man as a 'seeker' following in his father's footsteps.

... There is the young woman, still only expecting her first child, who sees the field and the path leading off into the distance, and there is the old woman she sees – leading by the hand those same three close-cropped children in the baggy shirts of the pre-war age; and herself, again, but now abandoned at the other end of the field of life, looking forward into the future that has yet to come about ...

The death of the mother in *Ivan's Childhood* is not only an image of catastrophe, it is also an image of destitution, of abandonment, of the loss of the natural birthright of maternal kindness. The theme of fatherhood would emerge later.[8] But even if it is not stated here in the most direct fashion, this theme *is* present in Tarkovsky's work right from the very start.

One of the bones of contention between Bogomolov and Tarkovsky was the choice of the actor Grinko to play Lieutenant-Colonel Gryaznov. Bogomolov wanted to see a real professional soldier, 'if not God Himself, His personal deputy in counter-espionage'. For Tarkovsky, Gryaznov was the man who wanted to adopt Ivan; if not his real father, then his personal deputy on the field of battle. From then on Grinko was to appear in all his films.

Tarkovsky had his favourite actors, as do so many film-makers. Every director has his favourite faces, too. Tarkovsky was much less interested in acting ability than in faces themselves, and often chose one from the people around him, even from the film crew; he proved surprisingly consistent in his tastes. For instance his production manager, Tamara Ogorodnikova, plays the mysterious figure in *Mirror* who appears to ask Ignat to read Pushkin's letter; it is also she whom we see in Chris Kelvin's family home as his father's second wife, or perhaps his sister. The director does not specify these family relationships. Evidently her face had a meaning for him that does not depend on links of family or plot; she appeared for him to express the idea of 'home', in the broadest possible sense.

The same thing can be seen in the case of Grinko, only much more clearly. In one way or another, his image was always linked for Tarkovsky with the idea of paternity, with the image of fatherhood if not with the father himself. In *Rublyov* he plays Daniil Chyorny, Andrey's mentor; in *Solaris* he plays the father. In *Mirror* his age was wrong for the part of the father, so the director moved him to the edge of the story, to the scene at the printing works where he plays the mother's boss. This part still retains all the noble, long-suffering paternal qualities that he embodied for Tarkovsky.[9]

On the other hand, the motifs of childhood, family relationships, of guilt, retribution and returning to the fold, are complex. They changed and were sometimes opaque, beginning with the repressive regime of the mother in *The Steamroller and the Violin* and ending with the double image of the mother and wife in *Mirror*.

Mirror, in fact, seemed like a culmination of all Tarkovsky's previous work. It had come to fruition deep within him and emerged as the climax and catharsis of all these motifs. *Mirror*, with its minutiae of family squabbles and its eternity of fatherhood and motherhood, also brought to the surface something which had been implied in the earlier films. For Tarkovsky, family relationships were not localized and petty, but rather eternal and elemental, somehow universal. They were like the changing generations, stretching back into the past and also reaching forward into the mists of the future, trailing their blunders and their sins, but also their loves and aspirations, their striving and spiritual needs. Tarkovsky's motifs, even the least significant, are always reaching out toward the universal concerns that stand behind them, however loudly the director insisted that all he wanted to portray was 'the facts'.

8 · Space and Time in Tarkovsky's Work

> But still my homeward way has proved too long.
> While we were killing time there, old Poseidon,
> it almost seems, stretched and expanded space.
>
> Joseph Brodsky[1]

Time was the key concept for Tarkovsky's whole approach to cinema. He came of age during that memorable period when the basic principles of the cinema, like its montage structure or its narrative function, were being questioned for the first time. Observation was then the dominant idea and we were at last able to read (somewhat belatedly) in Russian the work of André Bazin and discover his conception of the cinema as 'mummified time'.[2]

In 1967 Tarkovsky had written that, when the cinema was invented

> man received a matrix of 'real time' into his hands. The cinema is first and foremost imprinted time. But in what form does the cinema make this impression upon time? I would define the form as *factual*. If time in the cinema is expressed as a fact, the way we perceive that fact is through direct observation of it. The chief formal principle of the cinema ... is observation ... My ideal form of cinema is newsreel footage.[3]

Twelve years later, he would write:

> A natural difficulty arises here. Suppose I want the audience to feel that in no way am I manipulating its perceptions, I want it to put itself voluntarily into my hands ... But here's the paradox! The director's perception of time will always be felt as a *manipulation* of

the audience's perceptions . . . I therefore see my task to be *the creation of my own, personal stream of time, the realization on the screen of my own perception of the movement or flight of time.*[4]

Tarkovsky's basic understanding of the cinema remained unchanged: 'The cinema succeeds in capturing time in its external aspects, those accessible to the senses. That is why time becomes the cornerstone of any film-making.'[5]

In fact, it was only in the most philosophical sense that Tarkovsky's ideal form of cinema was newsreel footage. In practice, even the precisely dated episodes of *Andrey Rublyov* were variations on a theme: his personal perception of the subject, successfully made to look like documentary observation. Here, the subject was the fate of the artist. Over the intervening twelve years Tarkovsky, now the veteran of battles not only with bureaucratic procrastination but also with the very real obstacle of audience reaction, had not so much changed his views on cinema as adjusted his theory to bring it closer in line with his own practice. 'Real time', in his films, was always individual time, and it was the content of human ideas that he took as the 'fact' to be conveyed.

Indeed, Andrey Tarkovsky, though he may have changed the words in which he expressed himself, remained constant to his experience of the cinema, just as he remained constant in all else. Striving for the absolute is more a trait of character than of conviction. He did not know the art of compromise, of going half-way, either in ordinary life, or – even less – in art.

And as for the 'individual stream of time', in any film, even in newsreel, this will always be individual, for the camera singles it out from a broader stream – the stream belongs to the camera, and no longer to nature.

There are therefore no imminent laws of cinematography at stake. What one director hails as an 'ideal form of cinema', another will dethrone with equal conviction. When we talk of time, this refers to something much more personal: the system of conventions which any artist evolves for himself – in other words, the particular 'chronotope' to be discerned in the films of Andrey Tarkovsky.[6]

The inclusion of newsreels in feature films has become part and parcel of the cinema of today. We all live under the shadow of the documentary boom of the fifties. Tarkovsky, too, made use of newsreels.[7] In *Ivan's Childhood* they were part of the film's finale, and in *Mirror* they constituted one of the independent visual strata of the film.

Every film-maker knows that time in a newsreel and in a fictional sequence flows in different ways, but few make use of this fact when they splice in a documentary episode. For the most part, documentary footage is used for its symbolic power, or as an element of style, but far more rarely does it serve as direct evidence of the events portrayed.

The difference of scale between historical time and personal time in *Mirror* is almost unique in cinema. The strange, pulsating rhythm of time in the film is created by the flicker of the old newsreels. What might be seen in the cinema of today as a logical or aesthetic feature is, in this film, the determining factor for the form. This, in its turn, is to a very large extent a function of the particularities of Andrey's Tarkovsky's chronotope.

In this chronotope the past always exists on an equal footing with the present; the world of the imagination coexists with the real world. It would not be an exaggeration to say that these are as real and as present as the elements of the actual plot.

In so far as many kinds of retrospection, digression and interior monologue are commonplace in the cinema of today, audiences have long ago learned to read their visual language and face no difficulty at all when confronted by them. What we are dealing with here, however, is not merely a flash-back of the type when the younger brother in *Rublyov*, leading the Tartar attack on defenceless Vladimir, remembers being forced into an unwilling reconciliation with his older brother. A recollection of this kind is part of the plot, part of the chain of cause and effect, and therefore an integral part of the temporal continuity.

What Tarkovsky presents as dreams, as imaginings, as memories, even as flashes from old newsreels, is the element in which a character exists and has his being, is his 'individual stream of time' that exists alongside the time of the plot. In this scheme of things all moments in time are co-equal, existing alongside the ostensible plot.

In 1967, when asked about dreams, both waking and sleeping, and about the sequences where a character's attention is directed inwards, Tarkovsky answered forthrightly: 'Dreams depicted on the screen must consist of elements as sharply visual as the natural forms of life itself.' In *Mirror*, as in *Solaris*, he moved away from this ascetic declaration, but as always he remained true to the most essential: that which the hero sees when looking inwards is as real and as significant for him as all the ramifications of external reality. It was the same for all Tarkovsky's heroes, right from the first, from the little violinist whom the music-teacher reproaches for his 'dreaming'. And however naturally the 'waking dreams' are introduced into the plot, they always differ in one essential way from the 'naturalness' of the rest of the film: their time and space are from the realm of the imagination, and independent of the time and space contained within the framework of the plot. The two are in direct confrontation.

Tarkovsky was always extremely concerned with the physical, sensory forms in which the action of the film takes place. When the subject was the fifteenth century, the prop department practically exhausted itself in its efforts to satisfy the director's exacting requirements. He himself, however, was forced to recognize the limits to 'naturalness': he was well aware that 'his' fifteenth century would remain the fifteenth century of a twentieth-century mentality. This is why the magnificent sensory texture of *Andrey Rublyov* is built up from simple, accessible, tangible materials and objects and not from those found in museums and archives: milk and bread; canvas; sheepskin and fur; log walls; white stone and plaster; apples and cabbage; firewood.

The object-world of the film is clear and visual. It may be set in the distant past, but it is nonetheless not detached from the present. It is contemporary, but in no sense 'brought up to date'. And, of course, the same fields, clouds and sky, forest paths and rivers still exist; they are eternal when set against the life of man. The great world of nature will always be the setting for cinema. But for Tarkovsky there was also his own little world of nature, his individual world, and it was in this individual world that the particular qualities of his chronotope were clearly defined.

Andrey Rublyov is the most objective of his films in the sense that it apparently has least to do with man's inner world and nothing at all to do with childhood. This is, however, an illusory impression. According to the original script:

> Andrey, as a little boy, jumped into the cold, translucent lake; the shimmering tree trunks stretched their roots right down to the ghostly bottom, shadowed with swaying weeds; a startled carp darted away with a gleam of dull gold from its scales; a trail of bubbles from a lone bivalve shell was suddenly mingled with another trail . . .
>
> Then he remembered flying downhill on a sledge, his eyes burning in the wind . . . The whole hill was covered with boys and girls; the black trees rushed to meet him, and beyond them lay the white veil of the winter river, its blinding surface criss-crossed by the dark line of the road and the black water-holes where the women were rinsing the clothes; and down below, as children played sacks-on-the-mill, he braked in the middle of the river, covered with sparkling white rime; and a shaggy dog, its coat still covered in tares from the summer, stood torn between conflicting desires to jump on his chest or to lick the hot, laughing face of a little girl who had managed to crawl out from the pile of children on the crunching snow in the middle of the river . . .

Of course, Rublyov's memories of his father and mother never passed beyond the paper stage. But these simple, spontaneous scenes of nature, in its summer and winter variations, were not to be lost for ever – if they escape from one film, they resurface in another – at the start of *Solaris*: the green depths of an expanse of water; the swaying weeds; an orange bivalve shell, leaving a long silver trail as it floats to the surface. These 'facts' have emigrated from *Andrey Rublyov*.

The same sequence supplied an episode for *Mirror*: a small boy scrambles up a snowy slope. When he stands at the top, the view opens out into a Brueghel-like scene with tiny figures of people and a miniature horse. A great glittering expanse stretches behind; a bird flies down across the picture on to his shoulder.

The plot may change, or the camera position, or the angle; but the scene remains unchanged, as though it had been stored up somewhere long before the film was ever planned. It was already there in the artist's inner world, ready to appear later, having come to the surface as part of another film. No matter that the action of *Andrey Rublyov* takes place in the Russia of the fifteenth century and that of *Solaris* in the indeterminate future. The trail from the shell is independent of the chance circumstances of time and place. It exists *for ever*.

And so does the hill with human life scattered across its steep breadth. This 'for ever' pushes through the flickering newsreels that bear an exact date – Russian tanks in Berlin, Hitler's corpse, the deadly mushroom of Hiroshima or Mao on Tiananmen square in Beijing. If the minor time of human lives rubs shoulders in the film with major time – the time of history – then this concrete, historical time is measured in turn against Time itself – where a hillside can migrate from the fifteenth century of *Andrey Rublyov* to the twentieth century of *Mirror*.

It is not, of course, these chance migrations that are of the essence: they are merely the most vivid embodiment of that which is peculiar to the chronotope of Andrey Tarkovsky. The 'subject time' into which is fitted this or that aspect of an individual's or a people's history is always, in his work, synchronous with the *whole* of Time, stretching away in all directions untrammelled by limitations.[8]

This fact was often consciously recognized by the director as the link between generations, itself a special form of 'lived' time. As Arseniy Tarkovsky reads from his poem in *Mirror*, 'I will summon any of the centuries', so his film-maker son could leap from the fifteenth century to the science-fiction future. The father says, 'The table, same for great-grandsire and grandson', while Andrey demanded that the unmade scene of morning on the Kulikovo battlefield should be transplanted from *Andrey Rublyov* to *Mirror*.

But the director realized that the Kulikovo battlefield scene was simply not compatible with the texture of *Mirror*, and so had to give up the idea. But in contradiction to his own stated idea of the film as an 'observation', he persisted in translating this visual idea, evidently so dear to him, into a verbal one, and introduced the scene (so puzzling to many in the audience), of the reading of Pushkin's letter to Chaadayev.

The truth is that verbal quotations, even from Pushkin, are not essential to the film, for this feeling of 'the whole of time' is as present in *Mirror* as it is in the rest of Tarkovsky's films. It is linked, in part, with the theme of art in its broadest possible application.

Tarkovsky refused to recognize any such thing as special film music or to accept that there could be any independent role for the art director in the cinema. He used to look ill if he heard the cinema referred to as a 'synthetic' art form. This is not surprising if we remember the firmness of his ideas not only before he began work on any particular film, but even before he came to the cinema at all. These ideas could, in principle, have been expressed not only in film, but in any other medium as well. If the cinema of the future is ever freed from all the encumbrances of equipment and the need to co-opt a multitude of specialized personnel, if it ever comes near to the idea of 'camera-stylo', Tarkovsky is the film-maker who pointed most clearly in that direction in our day.[9]

But if he refused to recognize the art director as an independent artist in the cinema, art itself is always there in his work as one of the essentials of his world, one of its co-ordinating points, the counterbalance to the newsreels. Newsreels are merely real: art is eternal.

Dürer in *Ivan's Childhood* is not only an expression of the link between different ages: he also embodies the *whole* of human time. It is significant that little Ivan does not even notice the artificiality of the medium in which Dürer works, but takes his Horsemen of the Apocalypse literally as Germans that the artist simply happened to see and draw.

The pre-revolutionary volume of Leonardo in *Mirror* is not only an authentic part of pre-war life, but also a window on to a perspective which looks back down the centuries. Both Solovyova, the doctor's wife, and her cherubic baby dressed in lace take on for Alexey the mock-seductive aura of a Renaissance painting. Newsreels of the war are engulfed in the depth of time when set against the majestic resonances of Bach and Purcell. In *Solaris* the inhabitants of the station, both separately and together, exist against a background of reminders pointing to the pinnacles of human culture. Pictures of the *Trinity* and of Echmiadzin are part of their personal possessions; a mask of Beethoven, a bust of Socrates and the Venus of Milo stand in the library; and they have the music of Bach, to whom Tarkovsky will return in *Mirror*. He, too, moves from film to film, for he is no less infinite and eternal than the trail of the shell on the surface of the water. Culture belongs to the *whole* of human time.

And Brueghel. The long, slow panorama across all the details of Brueghel's 'Winter' that would seem to be Hari's substitute for personal acquaintance with the Earth could serve as a pattern for the sense of space in Tarkovsky's films.

Space in the cinema is something far more closely tied to physical detail than is time. It is achieved by the depiction of a particular place in a particular age and under particular circumstances. It can be seen to be northern or southern; the land can be worked, or shaped, or populated in some specific way. And Tarkovsky, devoted to the 'fact', was always scrupulous about this.

For instance, the flight motif is the embodiment in Tarkovsky's films not only of the characters' psychological state, but also the physical means of achieving that 'Brueghelian' angle of vision, which embraces the whole of the world; an image of the *whole* of space, whether seen from flight over the earth or from the depths of space. And if the 'subject' time in Tarkovsky's films is synchronous with the whole of human time, so is the 'subject' space in which the action takes place commensurable with the whole of human space.

The action of the subject can usually be dated exactly, not only by what is taking place, but also by the objects and places, by their physical texture, through which the story unfolds. Nowadays the type of glass jugs for flowers that feature in *Mirror* no longer exist; if they do reappear in *Solaris*, this amounts to Tarkovsky paying his dues to his ancestral memories. A well with a shadoof is no rarity, but exactly the same well appears in *Mirror* as in *Ivan's Childhood* – it came to both films from the same land of memories.

And this is what gives the events recounted in Tarkovsky's films their quality of *everywhere* and *always*. They belong to the objective world of things, but also to the inner world of man, which encompasses all things.

The linguist Vyacheslav Ivanov has written in 'Even and Odd' that in many languages the possessive pronoun has the broader meaning of 'mine, inseparable from me'.[10] The languages express spatial relationships in the same way: 'above me' would be expressed by the concept 'mine, upwardly inseparable from me' and so on. This type of possessive pronoun would be the perfect way to describe the particular quality of Tarkovsky's chronotope, inseparable from the author's self and embracing the whole universe.

And if an artist who claimed no desire to tell a story was apparently so willing to work in the science-fiction genre, might that not be because in this, as in no other type of film, he was free to create his own, personal chronotope, and so choose which physical events and details he would include while retaining the freedom to explore the limitless potential of the human imagination within those twin abstractions classified as 'everywhere' and 'always'?[11]

9 · Cinema as Poetry

It's the full-throated shrill of a whistle,
It's the crack of two ice-floes colliding,
It's the night as it freezes a leaf,
Single-combat of nightingales' song.

Boris Pasternak[1]

All Andrey Tarkovsky's films, with perhaps the exception of *The Steamroller and the Violin*, created some kind of sensation when they were released, even among cinema professionals quite familiar with innovations from the rest of the world. Each time, the film would gradually ease itself into the current repertoire and continue to attract audiences long after the sensation had ceased to be a draw. Of course, it is the director's name that draws the audiences. But there also seems in these films to be something, some kind of spiritual sustenance that feeds a constantly experienced hunger. After all, it is not for entertainment, or simply to kill time, that people go to see a Tarkovsky film.

If we leave aside the social factors and try to discover within the films themselves what exactly it is that attracts audiences, we must start with the narrative structure. In other words, if we ask the question 'How did Tarkovsky construct a film?' we will also be answering another question: 'What was he trying to say?'

The real 'how' for Tarkovsky was as little a function of subject, genre, or narrative forms as was the chronotope of his films. This sometimes proves a great disappointment: when, for instance, *Solaris* was shown at the Cannes Film Festival, many were indignant at its length, its sparsity of action, at the slow way the plot unfolded. What

CINEMA AS POETRY

determined their expectations was the genre of the film: if science fiction is to prophesy, people prefer it to do so in an entertaining and exciting way. But the one thing that never concerned Tarkovsky was 'entertainment'. His films always flow at that dignified, self-respecting pace that caused the events in the 'external' plot to dissolve in the stream and lose their crucial emphasis.

On the other hand, the structure of Tarkovsky's films always contained its own internal excitement, creating a field of tension between the film and the audience. It is this which gave each film in its early career a reputation for incomprehensibility.

I once saw a cinema full of science-fiction writers totally perplexed by the 'puzzles' in *Solaris*. They imagined that the fault lay in the plot, but in fact whenever a lack of understanding arises, it is always to do with what Bela Balazs called 'the optical language', the actual visual code of Tarkovsky's films.[2] This was always one step ahead of the audience, even professional spectators. Later, when Tarkovsky's grammar had been assimilated into the cinema of the day and become a part of it, the film would take its rightful place in the repertoire. But entertaining he could never be, for the essential excitement of his work lies not in what happens on the screen, but in this visual code. The topical and, therefore, impermanent elements – such as the expressionistic distortions in *Ivan's Childhood* or the violence in *Andrey Rublyov* – lose their shocking impact with time. But with or without that impact, the film still demands an effort from the audience, a spiritual effort. The more the form of the film prevails over the exigencies of plot and narrative structure, the greater the effort required.

Going back to that day we first saw *Ivan's Childhood* in that little viewing-room at the Film-Makers' Union, I remember the inchoate impulse, the hint of alarm and fragmentation with which we were left by the film. It was as though we had seen dark shreds of cloud whirling across the sky, suddenly illuminated by an out-of-place shaft of sunlight. Now, when I see the film again, I am astonished to find it balanced and complete, with each strand of the plot, every visual and other motif carried through to its logical conclusion in total clarity.

Take, for instance, one of the most harrowing images in the film: the bodies of Lyakhov and Morozov hanging on the other bank of the river. The 'Lyakhov and Morozov' theme is perfectly integrated into the overall plot with impeccable logic. They were the two scouts who crossed over previously to meet Ivan and were captured. The corpses were put out on the bank with the nooses still around their necks and decorated with a mocking placard bearing the legend: 'Welcome!' Kholin, for whom Lyakhov and Morozov were more than symbols crying out for vengeance, but colleagues and fellow scouts, and for whom the corpses therefore represent a personal threat, remarks irritably to Galtsev when he joins the battalion that the bodies should have been brought home. Later, when Kholin and Galtsev see Ivan over to the 'other' side, they load the corpses into the boat and cover them with a tarpaulin, leaving the two broken nooses dangling on the bank.

During the filming the author of the story insisted repeatedly to the director that it was ridiculous, from the military point of view, to combine the two operations of putting Ivan across and removing the corpses. No fellow scout would ever expose Ivan to that degree of risk. As so often Tarkovsky was deaf to the voice of expediency; in his image-world there was simply no room for two separate operations, but to leave this aspect of the plot unfinished, to reduce it to the level of an attendant circumstance, as in life itself, was also not possible for him. Bogomolov, for his part, could not appreciate the director's logic. However, for the audience, the 'Lyakhov and Morozov' theme is not at all developed with the consecutive clarity of the account just given. Such clarity is apparent only *post factum*, after an analysis which lies outside the film as experienced. The 'Lyakhov and Morozov' theme is, in any case, intended to create emotional empathy, which requires something quite different from military logic.

The hanging corpses enter the film as a sharp, emotional shock when for a brief instant they are highlighted amid the darkness of the 'other' bank by the periscope lens, accompanied by a sudden burst of percussion on the soundtrack. Their next appearance has even less justification from the plot, when – again, as a threat, like an exclamation mark of war – they burst in upon Masha's waltz. And as we now know, this juxtaposition between the waltzing birches and the hanging corpses on the other bank (which is the kind that normally occurs once a film has reached the cutting room) was, in fact, fully planned in the script beforehand, just as were Ivan's dreams.

Later, once the action has crossed over to the other bank, two ropes come into the frame and then, from behind, the two corpses. It is only at the very end of a quiet and terrifying crossing that Kholin leaves his companion, and the boat, now heavy, rocks upon the water, while sparse snowflakes fall upon the tarpaulin covering the terrible cargo; yet again, two nooses float into the frame, this time broken, and a last burst of percussion accompanies the dead men on their final journey.

Likewise, Tarkovsky takes Bogomolov's 'everyday' touch of the gramophone and uses it to build up one of the most poetic moments in the whole film, when the notes of the Russian folk-song 'Masha Must Not Cross the River' ring out and everything about it – the name 'Masha', the reference to the river, and the free outpouring of Chaliapin's voice – sharply and plaintively binds together the elements of the plot.

Tarkovsky was very much against the critical 'dismantling' of his structures; what he strove for was a smooth surface, not the dismemberment of his film. But since every work of art has a structure, and a film – even the simplest – is more 'structure' than many other types of art, the critic has an obligation to reveal the structures present. Such analysis, however, need not involve dismantling.

In *Ivan's Childhood*, which the director has often referred to as his 'apprenticeship', the inner, structural excitement that was to be a feature of Tarkovsky's films stands out particularly strongly. Each motif is developed and, although an effort of logic will sort them into a perfectly reasonable, literary narrative, we realize that this is not the point. For the overall movement in Tarkovsky was away from the narrative towards the associative; the logical sequence is broken down, the narrative links are loosened. This leads to a heightened accentuation of the visual 'optical' power, which in turn brings fullness to the motifs.

Someone remarked at the Cannes Festival that Hari's knitted shawl in *Solaris* seemed possessed of an almost magical power as if it had a life of its own. It is true; the shawl has its own plot-line in the film: we catch a glimpse of it in the first sequence on Earth, in a snapshot; then it materializes, together with Hari herself, in the cabin of the interplanetary orbital station; it remains forgotten on the back of the chair when Chris dismisses the first reincarnation of Hari; finally, there are two identical shawls on the chair since a 'second' Hari has appeared in place of the first. Like every motif in Tarkovsky's films, the shawl is experienced by the audience as an optical stimulation within the wider plot. Indeed, its white and brown wool and its hand-knitted texture really do seem to acquire their own independent existence, partly linked to that of Hari, but not completely so. Hari and the image of his mother both intrude upon Chris's subjective time (through photographs, on film and in his memories); for the audience the knitted texture of the clothes that both of them are wearing causes the images of the two women to merge even though the mother's clothes are in different colours, pink and white. This elusive melting similarity/difference between his mother and the woman he loved is signalled by the motif of the woollen shawl: the texture is the same, the colours different. This relationship is not something that could ever be expressed in words nor would it ever need to be. What it *needs* is a spiritual effort on the part of the audience, an effort to emphasize and to discriminate, and finally to perceive as a whole.

Ivanov has suggested that the difference between the functions of the brain's two hemispheres may be related to the semioticians' distinction between the components of the 'sign'. Thus the right hemisphere, which was also the earlier to be established, would contain our store of 'signifieds' in the form of visual images, while the left hemisphere holds our store of verbal and other symbolized 'signifiers'.[3] According to this schema, Tarkovsky could be seen as striving to beam his message directly to the right hemisphere, thereby evading the control of the later established, now dominant, left hemisphere.

Of course, this would be impossible to accomplish completely, and every member of the audience is bound at some point to call into play his or her interpretative faculties. Indeed, this interplay between intuition and interpretation is largely responsible for the pleasure a Tarkovsky film brings, however varied the individual's personal reaction to it; and it also helps explain why many wish to see the films more than once. The intellectual stimulation experienced by the audience after the visual trigger of the motif – even if this does not take place at the conscious level – gives the spectator a moment of true co-authorship, awakening the creative instinct. I am convinced that this is why Tarkovsky's films display such remarkable staying power.

This same evolution through which each separate motif passes also holds true for Tarkovsky's work as a whole. His earlier *œuvre* could be seen as the waning of external plot-structure and the corresponding waxing of internal content-structure: from *The Steamroller and the Violin*, where the narrative almost completely accounts for the content, to the complex structure of *Mirror*, where the associative content has all but squeezed out the plot of the 'confession'.

Likewise, the motifs are carried forward and developed. The similarity cum distinction between the mother and the woman once loved in *Solaris* is carried to its conclusion in *Mirror*, where one actress plays both parts.

When one views Tarkovsky's films in order, at least up to and including *Mirror*, they seem like one long film, divided into 'chapters'. The subjects, the stories that the film-maker is telling, are the variable parameter of the film, while the inner world of the author remains the constant. The subject is but the peg upon which to hang a revelation of this inner world, a world that is not merely a collection of memories, but a universe furnished with laws of its own. The elements within this universe are united by what Tarkovsky himself called 'rhythm':

> In the cinema a director expresses his individuality first and foremost through his sense of time, through rhythm. Rhythm gives colour to a work by distinguishable stylistic characteristics. Rhythm must arise naturally in a film, a function of the director's innate sense of life and commensurate with his quest for time.[4]

While the rhythm of Tarkovsky's films is invariably stately and solemn ('I want time to flow in a dignified and independent way on the screen'), the film itself is always brought into being through a changing pulse of rhythms,[5] new motifs flaring up and bursting in unannounced, clashing with other motifs and fading from the screen to boil up again in another part of the stream. The tiny sequence analysed above, with the waltz of the silver birches, the clash of the percussion and the corpses on the opposite bank is a fair example of the explosive nature of this rhythm. In all Tarkovsky's work, this 'individual stream of time' is something which pulsates, moves not smoothly but in jerks, in explosions of meaning, however hard the director insisted upon the amorphousness and simplicity of his images.

I once wrote in connection with *Ivan's Childhood* (which in many respects is the most straightforward model of a Tarkovsky film) of what psychologists, following Pavlov, have called 'the dynamic stereotype'. 'From idyll to catastrophe' seemed to me to be a dynamic stereotype which encapsulated the sudden irruption of war into the peaceful life and the striving for harmony which emerges anew after every total disaster. It is this striving which determined a finale to the film that could not be explained as a dream of the dead Ivan but must be the author's own.

Tarkovsky's next films, too, preserve the slow but jerky 'problem' rhythms and the same unchanging dynamic stereotype which the ancients characterized as *per aspera ad astra*, 'though trials to the stars'. Just as a single motif is built up from fragmentary visual elements into a coherent whole, so the complete film strives through fragmentation and contradiction towards a kind of harmony, a sort of absolute: the grand harmony of the *Trinity* rises from the sufferings and 'passion according to Andrey'; the Ocean responds to the suffering conscience of Chris Kelvin; at the culmination of *Mirror* the field of his mother's life is revealed to the inner eye of her son: she stands at one end of it, young and ignorant of what the future might hold, and again at the other end, having acquired the fruits of experience, she moves off towards immortality, leading her children, eternally young, by the hand.

The finale of any of these films does not arise as the natural consequence of what has gone before in the plot. It always emerges from the true elements of the film – the inner world of man – and is achieved through an effort of spirit that demands a similar effort from the audience.

The changing pulse of rhythm in Tarkovsky's films was always the pulse of that 'effort' of which Pasternak spoke. The *unchanging subject* of that one great film that he continued to make was the striving for the absolute, 'the effort of resurrection.'

For this reason – however much he may have disliked the term – I have no hesitation in describing the cinema of Tarkovsky as 'poetic'. It is poetic in that fundamental sense once proposed by the spokesman of the Russian Formalists, Viktor Shklovsky, when he wrote:

> There is a cinema of prose and a cinema of poetry, two different genres. They are distinguished from one another not by rhythm, or not by rhythm alone, but by the fact that in poetic cinema elements of form prevail over elements of meaning, and it is they, rather than the meaning, which determine the composition.[6]

In other words, when the straightforward narrative cannot contain the pressure of ideas awakened by the story, the necessity arises to work not in the prosaic, plot-centred form, but in the 'compositional', poetic form. This is what increasingly happened in Tarkovsky's films.

Part III : Beyond the Mirror

10 · The Soul's Landscape, After Confession (*Stalker*)

It was hard to imagine what Tarkovsky's next step after *Mirror* would be. Proust was among the names which came up, although another man's *'temps perdu'* was hardly likely to fire Tarkovsky's imagination. Moreover, *Mirror* had been a culmination of what might be seen as his search for a personal *temps perdu*. He had unburdened himself, pouring out on to the screen a diversity of feelings, focused through the prism of his own personality; we, the audience, strangely enough, experienced them as an expression of the life we all shared before and during the war, brought to life on the screen with a power that was almost magical. The childhood Tarkovsky depicted was immediately seen as their own both by the many people who wrote to him after seeing the film and by the many more who, even though they did not write, immediately recognized in the film their own memories and their own secret struggles.

Alas, the kind of film that seemed perfectly natural for a foreigner like Fellini (the author of such autobiographical fantasies as *8½*, *Amarcord* and *Roma*) was hardly acceptable from a home-grown talent like Tarkovsky. Perhaps if he had devoted *Mirror* to easily digested family anecdotes of the kind that are finding popularity today as a journalistic genre, more people would have been prepared to forgive him his 'confession'. Many, however, were frankly irritated by his abrupt rejection of any accessible plot-structure, and although the film did not lie on the shelf for years like *Rublyov*, its distribution was nevertheless fraught with complications.

The next film Tarkovsky began – working for the first time with

Mosfilm's Second Production Group[1] – seemed to promise a return to the science-fiction genre and to considerations of plot, about which Tarkovsky had recently seemed so high-handed. Much hope was pinned upon the fact that the basis for the screenplay was the Strugatsky brothers' novella, *A Roadside Picnic*.[2] The story tells of a closed reserve, the Zone, which marks the place where Earth has been invaded by some mysterious celestial entity. The Zone is heavily guarded, being full of booby-traps as well as temptations. Here, the normal physical laws of our Earth no longer apply: it is governed instead by the mysterious and capricious laws of some alien nature, transforming completely this otherwise ordinary-looking terrain. The Zone is a magnet for scientists, adventurers and marauders, all seeking the many strange objects to be found there, which can be put to a multitude of experimental and financial uses. The Zone has even given birth to a new, semi-criminal profession, that of the 'stalkers', illegal guides to its marvels and pitfalls. *A Roadside Picnic* is the story of one such stalker who combines, like almost all adventurers, a romantic passion for the unknown with the most basic self-interested cynicism.

The 'key' to the Zone and its most sought-after treasure is a mysterious golden sphere which can grant the finder his wishes. However, this sphere has a sting in its tail: the wishes it grants are not our conscious ones, but those of the much more powerful subconscious (an echo of the Ocean in *Solaris*); it fulfils, not our obvious, but our most secret desires. After many adventures the Stalker takes in yet another party of seekers with the intention of sacrificing them to the traps in the Zone and then wishing for his daughter to be healed. He sends to his death a young man with more spirit than sense, only to discover at the last moment that the wish of the latter was to have been 'happiness, gratis, for the whole human race'. So ends the story.

When they started work on the screenplay, the Strugatsky brothers decided against a direct transfer from page to screen. They changed both the structure and title, leaving only the science-fiction genre and the basic elements of the plot. Even the first version of *The Wish Machine*, as it was now called, had three people seeking the golden sphere: the Stalker, the Writer and the Scientist (a reflection of the

THE SOUL'S LANDSCAPE, AFTER CONFESSION (*Stalker*)

continuing debate in intellectual circles on the 'two cultures'). At this stage the protagonists still retained their own names and the Zone its science-fiction attributes such as the 'time-warp', which had already swallowed up one expedition, or the mirages which seduced the Writer with the promise of peace and freedom (he leaves his companions and remains behind in the Zone), or the green dawn, along with other signs and wonders. The basic theme of the story was retained in the plot: the Stalker sacrificed the Scientist (also referred to in different translations as 'The Professor') to the Zone and reached the golden sphere, but the prize which he carried home, instead of healing for his daughter, turned out to be useless wealth.

Once Tarkovsky was involved, the science-fiction aspect gradually began to disappear from the screenplay, with the journey transformed from an adventure into an extended debate. Never, before *Stalker*, had the text of a Tarkovsky film had such an important part to play. The most obviously 'cinematic' elements – the golden sphere, the green dawn, the mirages – were all abandoned; proper names were forgotten; the convolutions of the plot were straightened out. Nobody now died, nobody reached their goal, nobody even crossed the threshold: the three came to a halt before the entrance to the Place. The whole complex science-fiction edifice had been pruned back to a few of the original themes: the Zone, the Stalker, the idea of wishes fulfilled, the sick girl and the journey.

The screenplay was by now so far removed from the original story that after the film was released, the writers were offered the chance to have it published as a new work. However, this intermediate *Wish Machine* proved not to be the final basis for Tarkovsky's film, but an independent work lying somewhere between it and the original novella.

What followed was a process of *minimalization* – in the writers' discussions with the director, in the director's subsequent work on the screenplay, and during the actual shooting.

Although in many respects *Stalker* seems a continuation of the previous films – sharing many of the same production elements – with it, I believe, we also witness the onset of Tarkovsky's 'late' period, which was to add only three films to his previous four.

The publication of the screenplay in *Science-Fiction Anthology No. 25* (Moscow, 1981) showed not only the form the future film was to take, but also revealed the most important and decisive change it was destined to undergo on its way to the screen – a change in the Stalker himself. 'You know,' says the Stalker's wife in the writers' screenplay, 'my mother was dead against it. He was a real tough, the whole street was terrified of him. He was handsome, and sure of himself . . .' In Tarkovsky's re-working of the screenplay, this becomes: 'You know, my mother was dead against it. You've probably realized what he's like. One of God's holy fools . . . The whole street used to snigger at him. He was so pathetic, such a mess.'

Such a complete change in the main character could not fail to change the whole meaning of the film, to such an extent that the film is 'about' something completely different. With hindsight, of course, it is easy to point out that the tough-guy, the swashbuckling bandit, is simply not a Tarkovsky hero. If the exploits of little secret agent Ivan or of young Boriska coincide at times with Tarkovsky's lyrical self, it is because their obsessions are a kind of inner revolt against the limitations of childhood, of physical weakness and of impotence. If Boris had grown up into a self-assured master bell-caster, he would have lost all interest for a director who has no use for life's winners. Even in *Ivan's Childhood* he has more affection for the naïvety of Galtsev than he does for the derring-do of secret agent Kholin (which became another bone of contention between Tarkovsky and Bogomolov.) The icon-painter Andrey Rublyov doing penance (the first version of the screenplay was called *The Passion According to Andrey*); Chris Kelvin, a prisoner of his own conscience; the lyrical hero of *Mirror*, weighed down with the burden of different guilts – these were followed by the simple-minded, almost 'other-worldly' Stalker, as played by Kaidanovsky, a new but very 'Tarkovskian' actor.[3] We should not forget that Tarkovsky had thought of filming Dostoevsky's *The Idiot*, and that there is a very strong tradition in Russian culture of the hero who is humiliated and despised.

On the other hand, it is equally true to say that the figure of the Stalker, as it took shape in the film, wrought a change of emphasis in Tarkovsky's work, and consequently in his whole world, without which

THE SOUL'S LANDSCAPE, AFTER CONFESSION (*Stalker*)

the way would not have been paved for the 'holy fools' played by Erland Josephson in the last two films.

When *Stalker* was released, it seemed to me to be a transition. As I wrote at the time:

> The world of *Stalker* in its ordinariness, with its laconic, pared-down simplicity, is a world reduced to such a tense singularity that it almost ceases to be an 'external' world, appearing instead as a landscape of the soul, unburdening itself by confession. It seems that the complex tapestry of themes and visual leitmotivs that pursued the director for so many years, had finally been exorcised upon the screen in *Mirror* and could therefore be excluded from *Stalker*. For this reason *Stalker* seems much more whole, much tighter and more unified, than *Mirror* did. In other respects, however, it also seems much more impoverished than Tarkovsky's previous pictures. No longer are we aware of the vibrating pulse of life, bursting to emerge; the urgent sense of *being* that had always provided the chief delight and magnetic, optical power of his films. An apple, bombarded by fat rain-drops; horses on a spur of sand, quite inessential to the actual plot; a shell's trail of bubble on the smooth surface of the water; a sudden downpour; the motifs of childhood; the vague but significant interrelationships of maternity, fatherhood, the family; the chain of generations, stretching away in both directions of time; cultural successions; and the motif of flight. All the themes with which the other films were shot through suddenly dry up when we come to *Stalker*. The cinematic element is simplified, but it is also impoverished, almost to the lapidary glitter of a parable. The film seems a summary of his mastery of the medium, but bereft of that idiosyncratic quality, that is the delight of the *cinéma d'auteur*. *Stalker* seems a more 'theoretical' film, and perhaps for that reason it has a quality of lassitude, as though the artist had passed through a crisis and was now pausing to take breath before the next step.[4]

Now, looking back at *Stalker* from the perspective of the later films, I would still characterize it as 'minimalist'. Perhaps there had been a crisis, as it seemed to me then, but it also marked a transition: a sign that something was ending, and that something new was beginning.

This minimalism affected not only the plot structure, which had moved far away from the original temptations of the science-fiction genre, but all visual aspects of the film as well. Tarkovsky had never surrendered to the siren calls of what special effects could provide; but while in *Solaris* he was visibly struggling against them, in *Stalker* they are simply banished.

In *Stalker* the aesthetics of 'estrangement', of making the everyday seem unexpected, finds its most consistent expression, embodied in the counterpoint of image and sound which weave together to build an eerie space, more 'fantastic' than anything which could be created by special effects. Eduard Artemiev's work on the soundtracks of *Solaris* and *Stalker* is a true example of a composer subordinating himself selflessly to the whole, and what he has written is something other than mere music. The images are concrete, while the sounds are disturbingly abstract and strange: clangs, squeaks and rustles.

It is not only the fantasy of science fiction and special effects that are vanquished, but also the everyday verisimilitude round which the original science-fiction story was built (and which has always been one of the strengths of the Strugatsky brothers' work). The everyday truth of the framework of the story (the Stalker's departure and, at the end, his return home) are reduced to a minimum that is almost emblematic. Colour, too, which had always been an irritant for Tarkovsky in the cinema, is also vanquished. Not by a total denial (a black and white film in the Soviet cinema of the late seventies would have been a real eccentricity), but by toning down the colour to a minimal, almost monochrome blue-grey register. Any sequence in normal colour in this film works because each comes as an unexpected surprise.

Psychology, too, is banished. The actor's ability to create an autonomous character on screen was never a concern of Tarkovsky's, for whom actors were more of a medium: not for nothing does the hero of his confession have neither face nor physical form, and all we see of him is a hand, releasing the bird, at the end of *Mirror*.

Work on this film took an unusually long time, and was fraught with conflict. A laboratory mistake which ruined much of the material already shot gave Tarkovsky the excuse to break with his cameraman

THE SOUL'S LANDSCAPE, AFTER CONFESSION (*Stalker*)

and begin again almost from scratch. Now he was not only co-author of the screenplay and director, but art director as well, and therefore one step closer to his ideal of absolute and complete authorship. This probably accounts for the ascetic unity of style that so insistently pervades the film from start to finish.

Monochromatic images, flowing occasionally into colour. Nothing which even remotely resembles the future. The Stalker's wretched dwelling, with its one metal bed shared by the whole family, clinging to the back wall of a railway shunting yard, shuddering every time a train rumbles past. Equally untidy and unlikely for science fiction is the gateway into the Zone, reminiscent of thousands of similar and not particularly significant 'secret installations'. Far from being something from the world of tomorrow, this looks more like today, or rather the day before yesterday, rubbish-strewn and neglected, like a jumble of old things from a junk-heap. Even the notorious booby-traps, the famous 'wonders' of the Zone that stand like milestones on the journey, show no signs of the marvellous, let alone anything 'sci-fi' in their manifestations, but suggest rather a moribund monotony. The most dreaded of these, the feared and hated 'meat-grinder', turns out to be nothing more than a long, leaden-grey pipe of the kind used by tidy-minded town planners to channel underground rivers and streams. Getting through it is a spiritual or psychological trial of strength rather than a physical one. Another of the traps is an equally mundane looking stretch of sand. Broken, twisted railway tracks, odd corners of dilapidated buildings, broken bricks, a floor with neither walls nor roof, ruin after ruin – all this evokes a landscape all too familiar to anyone who remembers the war.

Tarkovsky regarded an infinitesimal dislocation of the everyday as more threatening and frightening than anything a cunning property-master or special-effects team could ever produce. Suddenly and incongruously, for instance, an ancient telephone rings in the empty, long-deserted ruins. For Tarkovsky, the techniques of terror (for creating a truly chilling Future) are those of estrangement, and ambiguity – not the inexplicable, but the unexplained – sliding into the unsteady sphere of suppositions. The black dog that attaches itself to the Stalker in this dead zone where the only signs of life are the distant voice of a cuckoo or the squeak of some other bird is not, of course, a Faustian poodle, but an ordinary mongrel. Even so, in its silent appearance there is a hint of warning, like a distant echo of some half-forgotten legend.

In *Stalker* (just as in *Solaris* before it) there are few scenes of conventional science-fiction fantasy, and those that do exist are not what remains in the viewer's imagination; what we remember is more likely to be the modest little valley suddenly seen in colour by the travellers, a valley of grass and insignificant wild flowers. The characters speak of a 'wonderful field of flowers', but this is simply because within the oppressive and silent emptiness of the Zone it alone has retained its modest naturalness.

The film is ascetic and concentrated with no digressions, no flashbacks, no inkling of any other life the characters may have led. First and foremost this is a tense, spiritual journey: for the three of them it represents the path to a new self-knowledge. Much of the film is shot in close-ups, with the language of face and body expressive to the highest degree, though sometimes so stylized as to seem more of a line-drawing than a work of photography. Once again, Tarkovsky used two of his favourite actors, Solonitsyn and Grinko (the Writer and the Scientist) but he placed even more trust in the new actor, Kaidanovsky, who played the Stalker. While the Writer chatters compulsively about the meaning of life and death (his own shallowness is demonstrated by the self-interest and stupidity he always assumes to be motivating his travelling companions), the Stalker emerges as something very different from the swashbuckling adventurer the others take him for. He stands forth as an apostle and martyr of hope, striving to lead his clients to the miraculous room and to bring them the chance of having their wishes fulfilled. His face and body, photographed with an astonishingly expressive power, have been drained by previous, useless, attempts until they match the emptiness and flatness of the landscape in the Zone. There is a painful, unfinished quality about him, a feeling of great human potential unable to find realization and therefore doomed to wretched uselessness. He is an embodiment of the search for meaning, a supplication that remains unanswered at the end of the journey.

THE SOUL'S LANDSCAPE, AFTER CONFESSION (*Stalker*)

Of course, Christian symbolism has now become fashionable even on the Soviet screen.[5] For Tarkovsky, however, starting with the ruined church in *Ivan's Childhood*, this symbolism has developed naturally in its ethical, not to mention its properly religious, significance. The motif of the Trinity was already implicit in the story of *Andrey Rublyov*. In *Stalker* it becomes a visual motif again, with trinities of one kind or another in many of the sequences. After the roofless and defiled church, there is the fragment of the Ghent altar-piece beneath the water in the Stalker's dream; around it swim fish, a symbol for the Christ who has been with the Stalker both night and day. There is nothing coincidental about the Christian associations here; they are a part of the author's conception.

At last the travellers reach the long-awaited, and perfectly ordinary-looking, ruins. The tiled floor and broken syringes remind us of a laboratory and of the possibility that perhaps this Zone had nothing to do with outer space, but that the destruction might have been the result of purely human experiments. Once there, none of them finds within himself enough power of thought, passion or desire to test out the mysterious forces, in which, as it turns out, they do not even believe very strongly. The Writer fusses for a bit and then retires, and the Scientist defuses the bomb that he has risked so much to carry laboriously into the Zone. Gazing within themselves at the very threshold of being, they realize their poverty of spirit and cannot bring themselves either to give life to their wishes, or to test their shaky faith. In fact, the director makes very little of the legend of the miraculous room which can grant all desires, and it looks as unimpressive as does the rest of the Zone; moreover, the only example we are given of its effectiveness is in the story of Porcupine, the Stalker's teacher, who is in himself an interesting figure in as much as he never appears on the screen, but is created entirely through the words of the other characters. A character who exists only in words is something new in the cinema of Tarkovsky. His presence in this story of the journey is like a warning sign of spiritual defeat. So in the end the Stalker, the eternal apostle seeking his Christ, returns yet again dissatisfied to his humble dwelling, his wife and his sick daughter.

Tarkovsky's constant motifs are to be found within this film, but reduced, cut down, within the minimalism of which we spoke before. Against the backdrop of the overall style of the film they stand forth incomplete, and sometimes dislocated. But we see that the elemental framework upon which all of Tarkovsky's previous films were built is still there, even if reduced to a fleeting glimpse of the natural world in that ordinary valley. The proud, free beauty of his wild, unfettered horses, embodying the spirit of Nature, are echoed in the steps of the black mongrel as it picks its way out of the Zone after the Stalker and remains outside, among people, a natural and yet mysterious presence. And looking back, you realize that there was flight too, in the sweeping whirl of the camera over the Stalker as he lies huddled in the water. The Stalker's dream is one of the most beautiful and significant episodes in the whole film. Family relationships and childhood are also there, though the director adhered strictly, with no digressions, to the line of the plot.

The monologue delivered at the end of the film, straight to camera, by the Stalker's wife (Alisa Freindlikh) is perhaps the strongest part of the film, for unlike the short-sighted seekers after the meaning of life, she is motivated by the simplest, most concrete and unfeigned of all emotions: love. And the camera, which had focused so long and closely on the trio of seekers with their strained poses and their faces drained of life, seems to relax as it comes to rest on the face of the sick girl, so serious and so full of hidden life.

The films of Tarkovsky, the expression of his world, always leave audiences free to make their own interpretations and to relate them to their own lives. I find unconvincing the words that the director wrote about the telekinetic potential of future generations at the time of the film's completion.[6] I prefer to retain my freedom to interpret what is strange and ambiguous in the ending as the possibility of the 'fantastic' shining forth through the shell of the everyday world (for, after all, the moving glasses *could* have been moved by the vibrations from the trains rumbling past, even though this is not so in the film). For me, the gleam of hope in the little crippled girl lies not in her telekinetic abilities, not even in the advanced spiritual development which leads her to choose the poet Tyutchev for her reading matter, but in the

THE SOUL'S LANDSCAPE, AFTER CONFESSION (*Stalker*)

simplicity with which she pronounces words which are beyond the grasp of her elders.

The last scene of the film reminds us, perhaps, of the end of Fellini's *La Dolce Vita*, where an angelic girl stands for the ideal that Marcello glimpses, but cannot reach. Here, the camera comes to rest on the face of the sick child and her thin, girlish voice gives a careful and convincing rendering of Tyutchev's most unchildish verses. Suddenly we understand what was missing out there, in the derelict emptiness of the film's landscape.

> . . . through lowered lashes,
> The faint and heavy fire of longing.

The fire of longing, however faint, however heavy. But without that fire no stalker can show us the way, and no power – worldly or otherworldly – can respond to the vague yearnings that are dissipated by the wind.

Love, poetry and art: the eternal supports of the human soul, even when, to quote Tyutchev again,

> . . . crouched in the dust,
> It trembles in pain and impotence.

By reference to the world of childhood, Tarkovsky's world is once again defined, or rather its inner meaning is confirmed.

And so we might have ended this chapter on *Stalker*, which not only brought fame to Tarkovsky in the West, but also brought him into the ranks of those directors throughout the world who were filming apocalyptic visions. However, within a short time his film was to prove prophetic in the most literal sense of the word.

Previously the word 'zone' had for Russians an association with the camps and Siberia; but in 1986 it was to acquire exactly the same meaning as it has in the film, i.e. the site of a catastrophe. Suddenly, our television screens were filled with ruination caused not by any war and with landscapes more fantastic than any wonders of the silver screen: empty homes and gardens, and forests where no human foot would ever be allowed to tread. There was the frontier of the Zone, and there were the first – well, not exactly stalkers, but peasants stealing into the Zone to pick tomatoes or catch fish in the dead water, since the human imagination cannot encompass a danger that is intangible and invisible to the eye. And now the name of Chernobyl has become enmeshed with apocalyptic echoes and associations – including the star of Wormwood, falling to the ground.[7]

11 · From Confession to Sermon (*Nostalgia*)

Tarkovsky made *Nostalgia* in Italy. At the time he had no intention of remaining abroad: all the more remarkable, then, is the way he described the 'Russian disease' before it became his own fate as well. After *Nostalgia* the crisis that had found chaotic expression in *Stalker* became something clear and articulated. Artist by vocation and moralist by nature, he was changing, becoming more and more a moralist by vocation. He was defending his aesthetic credo: the act of recording time (even at the expense of reality within his films). As time moved on, so the basis of his work was changing, without changing anything in the artist's attitude to the world around him. Everything else receded further and further into the background in the face of his growing sense of the messianic role of the artist within the world. *Stalker* was the Russian-made introduction not, perhaps, of a new subject (for the director's themes and motifs remained consistent right to the very end) but of this new artistic premise, provoked by a new and acrid confrontation between Tarkovsky and Western civilization.

Although his talents were widely recognized and he was regarded as one of the cult figures of Russian art abroad, in the commercial world of the Western cinema Tarkovsky felt himself an outsider of a different kind – one who neither could nor would make any effort to change. Before, he had faced constant aesthetic confrontation in the bureaucratic minefield of his relations with Goskino; now that he was working in the 'anything goes' aesthetic of the West, he needed to rethink the ethical foundation of all that he stood for. Tarkovsky was not only against commercialized art; he was the very embodiment of all that was uncommercial. As an individual even more than as a film-maker, he was incapable of working to order, of adapting to someone else's standards, even if he should ever have wanted to.

The paradoxical position of being a cult figure, deprived of a sound financial basis, made it even more imperative that he rethink his position.

In his book, *Sculpting in Time*, Tarkovsky gives verbal expression to something which, from the very start, was encoded not just in the content, but in the very structure of his films – something which I once interpreted a quarter of a century ago as the 'dynamic stereotype' of the irruption of war into childhood: 'The violence wrought upon the inner life is total. But from this totality, from the practical impossibility of anything simply human, is born the almost unbearable spiritual longing for the ideal. From absolute disharmony emerges the dream of absolute harmony.'

At the time I wrote those words, neither the word 'spiritual' – now so hackneyed – nor the word 'ideal', would ever normally have been used by a well-behaved Soviet film critic. Under the chapter heading of 'The Artist's Responsibility' Tarkovsky gave his own definition of this longing for the ideal: the more hopeless the world depicted by the artist, the clearer his striving for an ideal with which to confront it. We thirst for harmony exactly because our life is so filled with disharmony.[1]

Such are the terms in which the director describes the meaning of *Stalker*, although these impulses were taking shape within him long before they found expression in either film or words.

In *Nostalgia*, made abroad and therefore somehow even more Russian, the structure completely matches the plot. The story-line, which Tarkovsky wrote together with the well-known Italian screen-writer Tonino Guerra, might well in other hands have become a suspense narrative or a penetrating psychological study.[2] It concerns a Russian poet Andrey Gorchakov, who is in Italy researching the life of the eighteenth-century peasant musician Pavel Sosnovsky, whose master sent him abroad to study music; he was a great success in Italy, but when he returned home, back to serfdom, he turned to drink and finally committed suicide. Andrey is accompanied in his search by an

FROM CONFESSION TO SERMON (*Nostalgia*)

interpreter, an emancipated though dissatisfied Italian blonde, and the relationship between them, especially against the background of the memories of home which torment Gorchakov, could easily provide the subject matter for a film in itself.

All these elements are present in *Nostalgia*, but their narrative potential and even psychological aspects remain deliberately unrealized, as in the director's previous films. Instead, the dilemma of the serf-musician is echoed in the hero's own life, a 'doubling' technique of which Tarkovsky was so fond; for him the journey to Italy became the same kind of journey into self-knowledge as the trip to Solaris or the journey into the Zone. We should note that the increasingly literary style which was evident in *Stalker* is continued into *Nostalgia*. Like Porcupine, Pavel Sosnovsky is a character who never appears on screen, existing only in words; we never see even so much as his portrait, although his unhappy life gives us a clear indication of the extent of suffering associated with being uprooted from one's native land.

The Italian film opens with a black and white Russian landscape and the keening death-chant of Russian peasant women. Suddenly we are back with all Tarkovsky's trademarks, the ones which seemed to have been finally pared away by the time he made *Stalker* – the wooden *dacha*, the unsaddled white horse in the long grass, the women and the boy moving from the edge of the frame into the distance, hurrying home, the dog slinking after them, the morning mist. This is not the family home of *Mirror*, unique and authentic; it is more an emblem extracted from that image, an icon of Russian life enshrined in the hero's imagination. The immediacy of the life being lived before our eyes which was so striking in Ivan's dreams or in the earthly epilogue to *Solaris* is no longer there; the reference to the past has become abstracted, and it seems quite natural that the sequence should gradually slow into complete stillness. Soon, however, we are back in familiar territory with the polyphonic structure to which we have become accustomed: only after the Russian prologue does the Italian present begin, in the shape of Andrey's bickering with his Italian interpreter on the mountain road in the tiny car and his irritable outcry: 'I'm tired of all these sickeningly beautiful sights of yours!'

In fact we see none of the famous sights of Italy; the film steadfastly refuses to offer us either what Gogol called the 'lure of exotic, distant places', the picture-postcard sights, the places that it would be natural to see on a first visit to *la bell' Italia*, or even the natural lushness of the southern vegetation and the picturesque bustling settlements of the *mezzogiorno*.

Although in this case we cannot follow the development of the film through the changing phases of the screenplay, there is a short television essay, *A Time to Travel*, made by Tarkovsky and Guerra in 1981 when they were at work on *Nostalgia*. From this we can see what Tarkovsky would use when he came to make a full-length film, what he was to reject, and what he was to retain for this, his first meeting with the richness of a new culture and landscape, using the same principle of minimalism that we witnessed in *Stalker*, whereby only what corresponds to 'the landscape of the soul' is permitted to filter through on to the screen.

There is no sign in *A Time to Travel* of the blue sky, the southern sun, the mounds of flowers, the steepness of the mountain roads high above the Mediterranean. Nor of the ornate magnificence of the baroque cathedral in Lecco with its remarkable mosaics, the alfresco feasting, or the villa in Sorrento whose locked doors might have opened to reveal the famous marble floor which seems to be scattered with rose-petals. We hear mentioned in passing the name of Gorchakov, because at one time the villa had belonged to some Russian aristocrat, but the name is all that finds its way into the film.

Few have been able to 'de-Italianize' Italy as effectively as Tarkovsky. The only local colour to find its way into the film is the procession of women, with pyramids and shining candles, carrying forth the figure of the Madonna, the patron saint of maternity and childbirth. But Andrey Gorchakov does not enter the chapel of Maria, Madonna del Parto, heavy with child.

Not for his eyes is the simple magnificence of the ceremony where dozens of birds fly forth from the Madonna's belly nor will he be moved to tears or laughter by these women's simple faith; he will not witness the clumsy efforts of Eugenia to genuflect, or hear the sternly muttered penance the padre ordains for a woman of today, chasing

FROM CONFESSION TO SERMON (*Nostalgia*)

after happiness without realizing that happiness is not what life is all about. All this bright stream of detritus from life will pass him by, and although it serves as the introduction to the theme of the film, the main character is left unaffected. The line of excision which can be followed through from the first of Tarkovsky's films, continues here in an unbroken curve.

Andrey is not even given the opportunity to enjoy contemplation of the Piero della Francesca fresco upon which the camera lingers for so long, upon the unsophisticated ordinariness and artlessness, the earthy reality, of this pregnant Madonna.

Later he will say that his wife is like the Madonna del Parto, but more beautiful, and the image of the pregnant mother will appear to him bathed in the radiance of sanctity. But this Tarkovsky hero will never enter the chapel for the sake of which he has travelled through half of Italy: he will remain untouched by the Italy of ancient stones, the cradle of civilization, just as he is by the Italy of the teeming villages and the life of the people.

In vain did Tonino Guerra try to tempt Tarkovsky with all the beauty of Italy: Tarkovsky remained deaf to the idea of a cultural programme for his main character and could not decide in which setting to show him, until one day he found himself in Room 38 of the little hotel in Bagno Vignoni.

In fact, *A Time to Travel* is a very Tarkovskian film. It allows us to judge not only what did not finally get on to the screen but also to see the material from which *Nostalgia* was born, to see with our own eyes the natural world being transformed into the images of the film.

The hotel room astonished the director with its strangeness: the window looked not outwards, but inwards on to the lift-shaft – a real setting for an inner crisis. In the end, this strange window, which had so astonished Tarkovsky, was one of the things which also failed to reach the screen, because he needed windows through which we could experience a powerful and apocalyptic cloudburst. The whole location was transformed: instead of the unpretentious pine furniture of the real hotel room, we see a stained plaster wall and the end of a metal bed, imported directly from *Stalker*, beyond which the open doorway into the bathroom shows us a round mirror and round-backed chair.

The discomforts of the real hotel room served as no more than a starting-point for the realization of that landscape of the soul which – as always in Tarkovsky – transformed external reality according to his vision.

But it was the emotional jolt he experienced in Room 38 that opened the director's eyes to the unsensational views of Bagno Vignoni and its unprepossessing moth-eaten culture. The high-ceilinged, deserted corridors of the old hotel, the healing waters in the pool of Saint Catherine, bubbling out of the worn-down reddish stone: these became the long-sought location for the action of the film.

The pool, too, looks different in the film from the way it looks in the documentary. The faded reddish tones are replaced by a leaden sombre colouring. Under the stern eye of Lanchi's camera the almost benign aspect of the old pool is transformed into something which appears unremarkable at the same time as it is reminiscent of Dante's inferno.

When Tarkovsky saw the first rushes, he was moved to tears of astonishment both at the quality of the material, and at the precision, (unexpected even by him) with which the dusky images reflected his own twilight inner state.

A Time to Travel presents not only those aspects of Italy which were to be omitted from the future film, but also contains a virtual catalogue of all the props that appear again in *Nostalgia*: the old lace of the curtains in Guerra's house, the unchanging mirror in its dark frame, the curve-backed chairs like skeletons of themselves, the dried flowers, the pile of empty bottles and, finally, the burning candle – the few solid objects that create the physical environment of the film.

Nostalgia, in the sense of a longing for home, a longing fuelled by an unsolved love story, makes up what might be seen as the first stratum of the film. Eugenia's readiness to embark upon a love affair is defined in her talk with the padre – she is a young woman, full of life and of unrequited desires, but a woman who feels cheated of all that simpler souls can enjoy, a home, a family. It is defined, as well, in her debates with Andrey. She loves Russia, Moscow, the Russian language and Russian poetry. For Andrey, however, her lively curiosity about everything Russian is as irksome as her understandable desire to infect him with enthusiasm for the beauty of Italy. The volume of translations from the poetry of Arseniy Tarkovsky which she carries around with her is for him a symbol of all that is untranslatable between one culture and another and of their mutual lack of understanding. Later, in his dream, the pages of this little volume shrivel and blacken on one of those bonfires to which man consigns his memories (as in *Solaris*).

The relationship between Andrey (it is presumably no accident that the director gave his hero his own name) and his beautiful interpreter, with his irritable outbursts, her petty jealousies and their bickering in the empty corridors of the hotel, could hardly be termed a 'love affair'. As in *Ivan's Childhood*, in the world of the later Tarkovsky 'petty intrigue would be out of place, while love remains an impossibility'.

In writing about Tarkovsky's films, one is constantly thrown back on the same definitions – not from laziness, but because of his remarkable consistency of subject matter. Apart from Hari in *Solaris*, love stories as such were not something with which he felt concerned.

Strange as it may seem, *Nostalgia* was not only Tarkovsky's first film made abroad, but also his first with a contemporary setting. For this reason we can see very clearly not only what there *is* in his films, but also what is not: what he erased when taking the imprint of time that was for him the work of a film-maker.

Everyday life has been expunged, not in the sense of the material world in which we exist (this has an almost magnetic sense of reality in Tarkovsky's work), but as the sum of relationships and interdependencies within that world. War was something with which the grown-up world could deal, at the everyday level, but there was no such acceptance for Ivan. Kirill, after trying to make his way in the secular world, is eventually forced back into the monastery by his inability to deal with the physical realities of everyday life in which Rublyov himself, whom we see dealing admirably with matters like cabbage, can feel perfectly at home. The purely human aspect of relationships, of who is related to whom and how, may remain unexplained in *Solaris* or *Mirror*, although any substitute motif is always developed to the full.

For almost any other Soviet film-maker not only the possibilities of plot offered by the relationship, however imperfect, with Eugenia, but also the empirical reality of the status conferred by the words 'official trip abroad' would have led to a stream of recognizable situations, either comic or sad. For Tarkovsky, the reality of passports, visas and officials, dates, official invitations, tickets and so on – apart from one point in the film, to which we will return – is practically non-existent. At the most, they are a peg upon which to hang reflections: 'They should destroy frontiers.' 'What frontiers?' 'Between countries.' The meeting and clash of cultures, languages and systems takes place in the inner, rather than outer, world, where Russia and Italy are personified in the two women, Eugenia and Maria, in two colour systems, black and white for the flash-backs and colour for the present, and in two musical styles, a single woman's keening and the Verdi orchestra.

If in waking life Andrey is irritated by the shock of contact with an alien culture, in his half-dream or imagination the meeting between Maria and Eugenia contains no enmity, but rather warmth. The women touch each other tenderly with outstretched fingers (a gesture from Renaissance painting) almost like an echo, a faint reflection of an alien culture which ever-so-slightly (as we so often see with Tarkovsky) changes nature and gives it an infinitesimal but tangible strangeness. In the same way the image of a pregnant Maria, rising, pale, is an echo of the visit to the chapel of the Madonna del Parto which Andrey never made.

Those who remember the Russian Golgotha of *Andrey Rublyov* or the recurring 'wife–mother' duality in all Tarkovsky's films will find a host of meanings hovering about these images from waking and from sleep: the pregnant Madonna by della Francesca, his wife Maria, the similarity between them (which actually exists only in Andrey's imagination), the Russian Madonna, all that she stands for: wife and mother, home and family, his native land – not to mention the apocalyptic rain shrouding the windows, spilling in to the floor, casting its watery shadows upon the stained white plaster of the walls, and the tortured shapes of the metal bed and the curve-backed chair seen through the doorway. We could go so far as to say that the inner world is exteriorized in this film, that we are shown Andrey's inner discomfort and confusion through the terminology of the hotel room, where we see him lying hunched uncomfortably on the bed, still in his shoes and overcoat, either asleep or semi-conscious.

At that moment, a dog silently enters the room (we do not know whether it is from the black and white dream, or whether it has wandered in from the street) and tucks itself in between the bed and the puddle of rain on the floor . . .

Now, Tarkovsky's work gives rise to an enormous circle of associations, and in this lies its attraction. It reveals itself to each separate individual in the language of his own culture and personality. However, if we are to write about Tarkovsky, it is necessary that we attempt to describe his world first and foremost in terms of his own films. If we *do* ask why the sharp-eared dog appears beside Andrey's bed, we must probably answer that it is as a mediator between two worlds, as in *Stalker*; in *Nostalgia* these two worlds are the Russian past and the Italian present.

The dog from the black and white dream turns out to be a mongrel which has wandered in off the street. Later we realize that it belongs to the half-mad Domenico, the 'voice crying in the wilderness' to local society as it gossips in the pool, a pool which seems to sprout talking heads and tight-laced busts.

With Domenico a new motif enters the film, the motif of the world's essential imperfection, or '*Weldschmertz*' as it used to be called, which gives a new resonance to the theme of nostalgia for home. It is also our introduction to an actor new to Tarkovsky, Erland Josephson.[3] In Tarkovsky's work a new face is a significant event, especially if it is a face which we are to see again, as we will Josephson's in *The Sacrifice*.

However, before we move on to Domenico, a few words about Andrey Gorchakov. He is played by Oleg Yankovsky. The role was intended for Anatoly Solonitsyn, an actor whom Tarkovsky had considered essential for his work ever since his first appearance in *Andrey Rublyov*. If there was no part for Solonitsyn, one was specially written, like the passer-by in *Mirror*. Unlike Burlyaev or Grinko, Solonitsyn was not for the director the embodiment of any particular 'idea'. Unlike Tarkovsky himself, he was supple, protean, adaptable, a real actor, and very much a man of today. His high cheekbones and attractively irregular features could convey the very essence of the artist Rublyov, open to all life's influences, or the icy fire of pure knowledge in the highbrow Sartorius: there was unexpected meaning in each new expression on that high-domed brow, and together actor and director carried out one of the strangest experiments with the role of Hamlet that the stage has ever seen (at the Lenin Komsomol Theatre), where the Prince of Denmark was depicted as so much the man next door that he even spoke in prose.

The untimely death of this man, not only an actor and a friend, but the true protagonist of the whole of Tarkovsky's *œuvre*, was an event which acquired an almost symbolic meaning for Tarkovsky, putting an end to a whole phase of his life.[4] Tarkovsky survived him by two films and five years.

Of course, Yankovsky, too, was not a new actor for Tarkovsky. He had been in *Mirror*, where he played the part of the father. It was not a large role, but it was important. However, he admits himself that he had to adapt the part of Andrey Gorchakov, and it shows. Yankovsky did not have the jaundiced scepticism that Solonitsyn could display or his self-mocking irony. Yankovsky appears still capable of life, not yet so eaten away from within that his death could be seen to come naturally without the character having to make a show of taking drops for his heart. It is as though, in his hands, the role has become more elegiac: one can imagine Solonitsyn in the same black coat he wore in *Stalker*, while Yankovsky's is herring-bone, almost light in colour. Just like the Writer in *Stalker* he never removes it throughout the film, reminding us of the shoes he has been wearing for the last ten years, or of the line of Tonino Guerra's poetry, 'A house is a coat' – which, after all, must mean the reverse as well: 'a coat is a house . . .'

The character whom Yankovsky plays is often seen from behind, sometimes in silhouette and almost always in shadow. Even when this technique does not efface him completely, it darkens him almost to the point of extinction.

In fact Yankovsky's Andrey Gorchakov, with his irritating jumpiness and the strange coldness of which Eugenia complains, is a seeker, like the Stalker. It is no coincidence that like the Stalker, he bears a physical mark: in the Stalker, it was a lock of odd-coloured hair; Andrey too, has a very distinctive white streak, like a feather fallen on to his hair, and by the end of the film he is noticeably greyer as it has spread over his otherwise black hair.

The crucial difference between the two films, however, lies in the fact that in the later one the seeker finds at last a man who is prepared to take upon himself the burden of the sorrows of the world and their redemption. This man is, of course, Domenico.

Erland Josephson now enters Tarkovsky's work not only as a new actor but as the embodiment of a new idea. His part will be to redeem, not once but twice, the sins of the world. His outward appearance would seem to promise nothing prophetic, much less sacrificial. He is a short, stocky man with a cultured, kind, and one is almost tempted to say 'nice', face; if he is a teacher, then it is definitely without a capital 't': a schoolteacher comes more readily to mind than a guru. There is nothing in any way fanatical about him, and yet the story much discussed around the swimming pool seems a terrible one: this man, reportedly a former mathematician, was supposed to have kept his wife and children locked up until they were liberated by the police. Like bubbles in the pool, the different versions and accounts are inflated further and further – fear? jealousy? faith?

We remember that such a thing really did happen fifteen years ago. We also remember the impression made upon us by the cinema of our youth, by Fellini's *La Dolce Vita*, in which the intellectual Steiner killed his wife and family to spare them the catastrophe of an atomic war.

It is not Eugenia, beautiful, lonely and childless, who becomes Andrey's centre of gravity in this new land, but this strange man who strolls around the pool with his dog and who asks Eugenia for a light, although he does not smoke – as we cannot help noting. Andrey asks her to take him to Domenico's strange house, something for which later on she can never forgive him.

Domenico's house is the third visual locus of this film. If the end of the bed was a visual emblem reminiscent of the Stalker's dwelling, Domenico's living-quarters are more a reminder of the ruins in the Zone: a half-demolished house, where the old lace curtain and the dried flowers are at best symbolic of a dwelling-place; where a looking-glass in the half-darkness of the spiders' webs gives a dim reflection of whoever has entered the door; where the floor is littered with empty bottles. Later, when the next bout of rain (Tarkovsky's Italy would appear to be as rainswept as his Russia) comes in through the holes in the roof, it will fall to the floor completely by-passing the upturned throats of these same bottles: an image of the dysfunction that reigns within the house.

In this crying desolation, set in the midst of the most beautiful of lands, Andrey will return to his thoughts about his homeland and discover the truth behind Domenico's story in a sequence where we see his terrified children and his wife kissing the boots of the policeman who is leading them out of the house, the faces of curious gawpers, all filmed as though it were an old newsreel, perhaps slightly slowed down. The only strangeness is revealed when we see the shining whiteness of the Grail beyond the parapet, revealing itself to the boy from whose lips is torn the cry: 'Papa! Is this the edge of the world?'

Here Andrey will communicate (in the literal sense, with bread and wine) with the mystery that Domenico is to reveal to him: he must carry a lighted candle over the water of the pool of Saint Catherine (a feat Domenico will not accomplish since he is declared insane and hauled out of the pool). The Christian symbolism at which *Stalker* only hinted, with the image of the fish, thunderously echoes forth in this film as Beethoven's 'Ode to Joy'. Andrey receives the stub of the candle and hides it in his pocket, and the talk returns to smoking, something Domenico never learned to do.

Naturally, Eugenia is no longer there to share this talk between men tormented by the sorrows of the world and by pity for others; she has lost her temper and stalked off, leaving Andrey to his madness.

. . . Suddenly we are back at the hotel, where Eugenia is drying her hair with her feet on his bed, back to her old accusations and the old quarrels. All such quarrels in Tarkovsky's films are equally unreasonable, incomprehensible and irrevocable.

The only realities are the strange, strident Eastern music heard coming from another room; the blood that will stain Andrey's nose after a clumsy slap from Eugenia (just like the blood on the Stalker's face – another sign of seeking in Tarkovsky's symbolism); and the dream of home which he will dream again, left alone at last.

FROM CONFESSION TO SERMON (*Nostalgia*)

In the structure of the film this dream of Andrey's mirrors the frightening dream-vision of Sosnovsky. Before setting off for Rome, where a 'real man' awaits her, by the door in the corridor Eugenia reads the despairing letter of the Russian musician. The serf's dream, although related in words, is also depicted in a black and white image: at his master's orders, he has to stand motionless depicting a white statue and can feel the deathly hardening of his legs within the whiteness and immobility of the plaster.

Andrey's black and white dream, into which an echo of a distant Italian melody has crept, interweaves with the frightening vision of the musician (here we see the double theme emerging in the fabric of the plot) and the dream is transformed into the half-waking of Italian reality. A strange crescendo of sound and a shock of colour makes a distinct break between this surrealistic semi-consciousness and the usual dream of home.

Amid their other qualities, Tarkovsky's films show a high degree of interpenetration, a quality one could almost compare with osmosis in the biological world. Independent of the time and place of the action, the themes, methods, signs and meanings flow over one into another, irrespective of the boundaries created by plot. It is no coincidence that words and ideas are so important in these films, where the most powerful weapon is not special effects, but imagination, and between the worlds of imagination and reality no visible boundaries are drawn, for both are equally truthful and equally right.

In colour, close-up: Andrey's silhouette from behind, as he retreats into the 'zone' of his imagination. This zone is astonishingly reminiscent (not in the figurative sense, of course) of the Zone in *Stalker*. In the earlier film, however, it was an external reality (at least from the point of view of plot); in this film it is, in the fullest possible sense, the landscape of the soul, where the same scene of desolation is reproduced, this time on Italian soil: the debris of human life goes on under a stream of water from above, a white, mutilated angel (a motif which has been appearing, in different forms, ever since the almost-obliterated fresco in *Ivan's Childhood*), the trail of an orange shell (an equally enduring trail, reappearing here from *Solaris*) and Arseniy Tarkovsky's Russian poems 'I Fell Sick as a Child' and 'Russian Still-

Life', heard under some Latin vaulting; then the bottle of Moskovskaya vodka, the plastic glass and the glowing fire on which the Italian volume of Russian poetry is to burn.

Sosnovsky's dream is a confrontation with Russian serfdom. Andrey Gorchakov's dream is a confrontation with the materialistic civilization of the West, in the person of Angela, the girl in wellington boots who appears from nowhere among the waters, like some local part-time guardian angel. Andrey claims to be tormented by shoes, by the mounds of Italian shoes bought by everyone, even though he has been wearing his current pair very satisfactorily for the last ten years.

We have already had occasion to note that from *Stalker* onwards, the text carries more and more of the ideas which give meaning to Tarkovsky's films. Not only characters, but stories and parables appear only verbally – including the parable of the man who was saved from a puddle, which he recounts to Angela: 'And there they are, lying on the bank of that deep puddle. They are panting, exhausted. Finally the one who was saved asks: "What did you do that for?" "What do you mean: what for? I saved you, didn't I?" "But, you fool, I *live* in that puddle!" '

Without trying to imitate Solonitsyn, Yankovsky found his own way into the part. Slightly drunk, his Andrey coarsens, but with a coarseness (sometimes naïvety) which can coexist with the poetry:

> I am a candle, that has burned in the world,
> Now you can save my wax for a feast

although the candle-stub given to him by Domenico is lying useless for the moment in his pocket.

This film, like all his others, flows naturally from the progression of Tarkovsky's *œuvre*; like all his films, it also fits perfectly into the mainstream of fashion in the arts today: the fashion for quotation, for self-quotation, for references, echoes, reflections and hints. His favourite pose, when Andrey lies prone among the waters as though he were a stone knight upon his own tomb, is a self-quotation; the wardrobe in the middle of the street, is a quotation from Bergman, perhaps by way of dedication (Josephson is, of course, best known as a member of Bergman's company). In the looking-glass, instead of his own face, Andrey sees mad Domenico's face looking out, a second

FROM CONFESSION TO SERMON (*Nostalgia*)

layer of *doppelgänger* in this seminal episode of the film, where 'nostalgia' is both longing for home, and the burden of the sorrows of the world.

And all the different possible meanings for the endless waters that flow through Tarkovsky's films: the Stalker's flight over water, Andrey's walking on water . . . And suddenly, with a quick flash of the editor's knife, the noise of a plane and a full, bright screen, almost like a picture postcard: Rome, seen from above. The journey is over, and Andrey is preparing to return home. A few short sequences convey the information with a directness that is almost vulgar: suitcase and packages in front of the hotel, signs of departure; the first conversation we ever see with the interpreter about practicalities – ticket, flight, official invitation; and for the first time instead of 'this Russian' we hear his name being used: Gorchakov. It is as though a window had opened on to a completely different, narrative film, the film we might have expected, about the Russian abroad, on official business.

And now, when the film returns to a normality of style, we at last become aware of the singular nature of time as it is captured in the work of this director. Tarkovsky worked with different cameramen, each with his own inimitable style; but each also, when working with Tarkovsky, produced a 'Tarkovsky' film, a particular fixed way of seeing with the eye of the camera. Sometimes the camera pans slowly; sometimes it just watches, neither scrutinizing nor inspecting the subject. The watching is leisurely, one could even say slow. In this slowness of observation lies the director's magic powers of visualization, as also in his microscopic slowing down of the motion and the tiny movements of his camera (and it is this, too, which creates the measured tempo that is so unusual for a Western audience). Time, in these films, does not correspond to everyday time: Andrey's journey to Bagno Vignoni could have lasted two weeks, or two days.

The scene of preparations for departure is filmed in everyday time, and for a moment we see the Andrey that we have known from his spiritual journey transposed into another reality. Then the telephone interrupts this everyday time of preparation: it is Eugenia informing him that Domenico has arrived in Rome and is now preaching, and asking if Andrey has kept his promise.

The sequence where we see Eugenia, less exotic now that we see her in contrast with the brutal mafioso whose face bears no sign of Slavic reflection, returns the film from the world of plot back into the space created by the subject. Andrey requests – with the permission of the Society for Italo-Soviet Friendship – that he be taken urgently back to Bagno Vignoni.

The dénouement of two lives, serving as each other's accompaniment in parallel montage, makes an unusually leisurely coda for the film, a coda which is perhaps the best part of the whole work. It is full of reminiscences, of consequences, of reawakened motifs, but it also contains something qualitatively new: the seeker finds someone prepared to show him the way.

Domenico is preaching on the Capitoline hill. The scene is reduced to its barest elements. A few figures, distributed statically and flatly on a broad flight of steps. Their faces bear the stamp of weakness, imbecility and mental illness. Domenico's dog is tied to the column, and Domenico himself has climbed on to the rump of Marcus Aurelius's horse to speak. He gives forth the passionate appeal of the sick to the healthy (a common motif in contemporary art): 'What kind of world is this? If those who are mad call out to you – be ashamed!' He calls upon his listeners to bring forth their souls like a sheet. Then he gives the signal, 'Music!' and one of the madmen drags a shiny canister over to Marcus Aurelius. Clumsily and none too successfully, Domenico pours petrol over himself. They hand him a lighter, but it clicks, unwilling to light in his clumsy hands.

And this brings us back to the motifs that weave through the films; if we look back we can trace the distinct, albeit sometimes submerged line of the inefficient lighter: starting with Eugenia's request for a light, continuing through the conversations with Andrey, when Domenico admits that he never did learn to smoke, and leading on to this final episode.

Nobody could destroy the glamour of prophecy and return the act of self-immolation to the world of prosaic, ugly and inept physical actions as radically as Tarkovsky succeeds in doing here. The lighter is an old one, it works badly; Domenico's clothing is unwilling to catch alight; when at last it does, he is cheated of a 'torch' effect: his clothes burn only at the back, creating a spectacle that is both ridiculous and painful to behold. The dog whines pathetically and pulls at its leash, and finally at last Beethoven's 'Ode to Joy' bursts out at full volume; the madmen, however, remain unmoved, except for one who falls at the statue's hooves in an epileptic fit and Eugenia whom we see running up the steps. Domenico falls from the statue with a painful cry and finally yields up his spirit, clinging to the stones face-down in a parody of the pose of a man crucified.

Meanwhile, Andrey arrives in Bagno Vignoni and, leaving his car, rushes to the pool.

Domenico's Roman sermon is punctuated by the carrying of the candle in Bagno Vignoni. A dog's whining, changing to a howl, unites the two episodes in one audio plane.

Andrey's Road to Calvary takes place in circumstances just as prosaic as those of Domenico's Sermon on the Mount, and is equally devoid of catharsis. The pool has already been drained, and on its edge stand various objects, covered in slime, that have been fished out of the mud at the bottom. Andrey will carry his candle not so much over the water, as over a layer of liquid mud. Like the thread of the lighter, so we can follow the thread of the candle (and, more broadly, the thread of fire) as it weaves in and out throughout the length of the film (Domenico's candle, Arseniy Tarkovsky's candle, the fire, etc.).

We have to appreciate Oleg Yankovsky's achievement in giving this scene, too, his own special stamp (if we remember, the rigours of the journey through the pipe in *Stalker* were conveyed entirely through the face of Solonitsyn, through his harrowed features and the suffering that gathers in his eyes). He gives his character a very prosaic heart condition so that he has to take drops every now and then. At first the enterprise seems not so arduous, so he lights the candle, and, touching the edge of the pool with his hand, sets off; the candle, however, flickers and goes out; disappointed, he goes back to the beginning, and relighting it, touches the edge with his hand again. So, it would seem that bearing a candle demands care: he shelters it with the edge of his coat, his feet slopping noisily in the mud; it would also seem that bearing a candle demands concentration: he moves so that it is protected from the wind by his body and walks on slowly and gingerly;

his hair no longer bears a streak, but a great fan of grey. Alas, the candle flickers out again, and, sighing, he weaves his way back again, stumbling, almost falling, and feels again for his lighter.

The sequence lasts a long time, without any cut; the camera is static, and gradually the audience is drawn into the extended action, as though into a vortex. By now, the bearing of the candle has become a giving of the self; he shelters it not only with the edge of his coat, but with his body and his whole being. The piteous whining of a dog is heard from afar; exhausted, he leans for a moment against some sort of ladder, sheltering the flame with his hands, and then sets off again. At last his hands fix the stub to the other side of the pool, and remain for a long time to protect the weak little flame.

... And then the splash of a fall, shouts, people running, the interpreter jumping from a car; then in a motionless black and white sequence, we see a modest Russian landscape, captured through the stone vaulting of a Romanesque church that has lost its roof, reflected in the little mirror of a piece of water – not even a lake, more a kind of puddle, and there sits Andrey with a dog. Snowflakes are spinning slowly, again a woman's voice is wailing, we hear a dog howling piteously and read the words: 'In memory of my mother. A. Tarkovsky'. And so the film ends.

Later, coming back to *Nostalgia*, Tarkovsky recognized the obvious metaphorical, even literary quality of this sequence as a digression from his own principles. But why does an artist formulate principles, if not to violate them? There is another curious thing: he had given preliminary agreement to the possibility of two different, almost contradictory interpretations of the 'model of Gorchakov's inner state', as either a fragmentation, preventing him from advancing any further in his life, or a unity achieved, allowing him to die having broken through to a new reality. Tarkovsky did not insist on either of these two versions: on the contrary, he relied on the multivalency of this visual expression of a spiritual state, merely warning us against other, external, interpretations. In fact, of course, not only this final sequence, but the whole film is open to different interpretations and the 'decoding' of individual motifs by the use of however sophisticated a system can reveal to us only a little of the director's intentions. The film as a whole continues to offer the possibility of many, and varied, perceptions and appreciations of all its different shades and layers of meaning.

12 · From Sermon to Sacrifice
(*The Sacrifice*)

What would be Andrey Tarkovsky's last film was made in Sweden. The fact that it was backed by various producers from different countries, as well as the main producer Anna-Lena Wibom of the Swedish Film Institute, bears witness as much to the esteem in which the name of Tarkovsky was held throughout Western Europe, as it does to the financial problems of the production. His name may have been a guarantee of prestige and quality, but it was no guarantee of commercial viability.

By this time his situation was radically different. After *Nostalgia*, Tarkovsky had decided to stay in the West. This decision was the outcome of many pressures. There was the memory of how *Andrey Rublyov* had been treated; the years of waiting, developing ideas which never came to fruition; his absolute inability to compromise; and the fact that not only were there continuing aesthetic confrontations with the Soviet film bureaucracy, but also, sad to say, antagonism from his professional colleagues. This last was clearly demonstrated at the 1984 Cannes Film Festival (where *Nostalgia* was entered by the Italians and, together with *L'Argent*, the film of his idol Bresson, was awarded the jury's *prix special*).[1] All this, Tarkovsky said repeatedly, right up to the last interviews, meant that it was not an academic, but an extremely concrete and personal nostalgia which, as he puts it himself, took possession of his spirit for all eternity.

All this came at a time when his audience at home was increasing steadily in numbers: *Andrey Rublyov*, *Solaris* and *Stalker* (although the same cannot be said of *Mirror*) were always to be found playing in some cinema, even if not the largest, and for the new generation Tarkovsky's film language held no terrors; indeed *Andrey Rublyov* has become one of the classics of the Russian cinema.

The Sacrifice was the first truly European film Andrey Tarkovsky made. He was already a very sick man, alternating bouts of work with periods in hospital, and in some respects the film reads like a last testament. More than this, however: with its elegant structure, its visual power, its compelling ideas and virtuoso mastery of all the means to express those ideas, it merits the epithet of a 'late' work in all the best senses of the word. No traces of weakness are to be found lingering in the film. It is a film which feels spacious, uncluttered, and somehow washed clean from within, perhaps also thanks to the camera work of the legendary Sven Nykvist, Bergman's regular colleague. Of course, another significant factor is the Swedish landscape, with its pale northern sky, low horizon and curve-edged plain on which you can see for miles – this plain landscape was closer and more penetrable to Tarkovsky than the southern beauties of Italy. It is true also that, consciously or not, Western audiences immediately perceived the film as 'in the Bergman tradition', which made them look for similarities. For Russian audiences, the associations evoked by the old house, the table in the thick grass and the wicker chairs, would be of traditional productions of Chekhov, in spite of the fact that the events which take place in the film, like those of *Nostalgia*, are happening in our own time, although visually they seem to have no connection with it. The film respects the unities of action, time and place in which Tarkovsky so rejoiced with *Stalker*. The subject matter, from the point of view of normal logic, is of course absurd, but it seems so natural an extension of *Stalker* and *Nostalgia* that we are surely justified in regarding these three films as a trilogy, even within the context of the one long 'work' upon which Tarkovsky was engaged throughout his life. Unlike *Nostalgia*, however, *The Sacrifice* is almost without direct references to previous films, although Tarkovsky's favourite motifs, whether they be of plot or subject, or the visual or ethical aspects of the film, are easily discerned.

Far now from Russian soil, the structure of the plot (although without direct reference to his own life) is made up of those motifs which remained so vital to Tarkovsky: the family and family relationships, fatherhood, childhood, home. Alexander, essayist, theatre critic and university lecturer, has stuck a dead pine-tree into the ground, accompanied by his young son, nicknamed Little Man. Little Man has a bandage on his throat: he has just had an operation, and is not allowed to speak although his father speaks non-stop.

It is not with this – a long static shot where small human figures can be seen bustling about the dry wood of the tree – that the film begins. As the opening credits gradually fade, we recognize behind them on the screen part of an old picture: the gesture of an old man, proffering a vessel, and the answering gesture of the infant in the arms of the Madonna; Bach's *St Matthew Passion* merges into the natural sounds of life – the cries of the gulls, the sound of the sea – that serve as a prelude to the landscape which is opening up behind the credits: a pale, flat sea, green flat fields, and a road meandering into the far distance, on which we can see the distant figure of Otto, the cycling postman. He approaches for what seems a very long time on his leisurely form of transport, and it is only as he comes up to Alexander that the camera moves, opening up new horizons in this monotonous landscape and more human figures, who approach slowly.

This initial sequence contains if not the 'intrigue' of the plot, then at least the knot of motifs out of which the film is going to develop.

The detail from the picture of the child, who seems to be accepting from the magi's hands his unique and terrible future (expressed in counterpoint with Bach's *Passion*) will develop, as always according to the inner laws by which Tarkovsky's films develop, into its own separate subject matter. From a puzzling, inchoate image will emerge a clear and concrete one: a reproduction of Leonardo da Vinci's *Adoration of the Magi*, which has been framed under glass and adorns Alexander's study, very much a part of the furniture and subject for conversations between the characters. However, part of the furniture though it may be, the Leonardo reproduction is never swallowed up as just one of the many objects in the house: throughout the film it will preserve its emblematic status, and many times the camera approaches it, peering into the disconcerting duskiness of the colours in which one of the most joyful events in the Gospels is depicted; the faces of

FROM SERMON TO SACRIFICE (*The Sacrifice*)

Alexander and Otto are reflected as through 'through a glass darkly', superimposed upon Leonardo's figures.

A list of all the times that the camera returns to the *Adoration of the Magi* would include all the important turning-points in the film, where the finger of fate is apparent. Indeed, we could take an even wider view of the significance, or rather the seminal importance, of Leonardo da Vinci in Tarkovsky's films: for instance, the battle scene in *Andrey Rublyov* is depicted 'in the style of Leonardo', drawing upon the latter's Treatise on Painting. Then there is the volume of Leonardo reproductions in *Mirror*, reflecting the ambiguous reality of the woman played by Margarita Terekhova. Equally significant is the fact that for *Nostalgia* – his Italian film – he needed not the multivalent, mysterious Leonardo da Vinci, but a Madonna by Piero della Franscesca, simple and affirmative in her earthly, maternal way – to whom Otto will refer in *The Sacrifice* in his otherwise puzzling phrase about preferring della Francesca to Leonardo (yet another manifestation of one of the general laws governing the work of Tarkovsky: their continuity of content).

For the present, however, it is enough to note the counterpoint between eye and ear that we meet in the prologue: the child being worshipped as future victim and saviour.

We should also note, for the larger meaning of the film, the silence of Little Man and the babbling of Alexander, with his predilection for asking himself 'accursed questions'. In the structure of *The Sacrifice*, as in that of all Tarkovsky's later films, the spoken word has a very important part to play. Not for nothing does Alexander say: 'In the beginning was the Word.'

And finally, there is the meeting with Otto, the postman (Allan Edval), who has sought out Alexander on his walk in order to deliver birthday telegrams from former colleagues in the theatre, which are signed in very curious ways: 'Your Richard friends' and 'Your Idiot friends'. The strangeness demands an explanation, and he has to explain that previously he was a leading actor, whose best-known roles included Shakespeare's Richard III and Dostoevsky's Prince Myshkin. Later, in the family circle, the conversation will take a new tack with an argument about his reasons for leaving the stage. The important thing for the moment, however, is that the hero of the film has tested his soul with absolute evil (Richard III) and absolute good (Prince Myshkin) and that these two, once played by him, stand on either side of the gates to his life and fate.

The meeting with this eccentric postman, a reader if not an admirer of Nietzsche and a collector of uncanny facts and experiences, is important for illuminating not only Alexander's past, but his future as well:

'And what is your relationship with God?'

'I haven't one, I'm afraid.'

It is Otto's ill-placed, casual response – 'Don't be too upset by it, and don't fret. And don't expect anything' – that serves as the catalyst of Alexander's inner crisis: 'Whoever gave you the idea that I was *expecting* something?!' In essence, the whole film develops from this inconsequential exchange of remarks.

It is also worth reflecting on the postman's name, for we may assume that it has a significance for Tarkovsky, since Otto was the real name of his constant actor Solonitsyn. The part of the postman, with his visible eccentricity and his invisible depths could not, of course, have been written for Solonitsyn – he was already dead – but it does seem likely that it was conceived in his honour, as a kind of memorial; the absence of something important, of some fundamental element in the world of Tarkovsky's films (a minus sign, so to speak) has always been as significant as a presence, and Solonitsyn had always been one of Tarkovsky's most powerful talismans. It is therefore not illogical to assume his invisible presence in the film.

When his wife and the doctor come for Alexander in the car, violating the rarified emptiness and peace of the landscape, and the hero of the film asks them to let Little Man and him walk on a little further on foot, in this lengthy, seemingly deliberately drawn-out introduction several more minor events occur that are important for the further development of the plot. One such event is Little Man jumping on his father from behind and being pushed off clumsily so that his nose begins to bleed.

The position in which Little Man lies in the grass to stop the nosebleed, and the blood itself, are the kind of punctuation marks in Tarkovsky's work which assume significance: here they seem to indicate a 'seeker'. And, in truth, Alexander, in the very first sequence of the film, tells Little Man the parable of the old monk and his pupil, whom he instructed to water the dry tree until it should flower. During the course of the film Little Man will imperceptibly take upon himself the role of just such a pupil.

Alexander, for his part, experiences (after the surprise attack by Little Man and the accompanying blow on the head) the first of those apocalyptic hallucinations which we can easily recognize as yet another variation on the theme of the Zone: we see in black and white a road littered with rubbish, water pouring down from some unexplained source, the skeleton of a curve-backed wooden chair, people running, and a house lurching surrealistically . . .

Abruptly, we pass from this litany of destruction to the harmony of a Russian icon: Alexander is leafing through a book he has received as a birthday present – a transition that may remind us of the *Trinity*, rising up from the blood and terrors of fifteenth-century Russia.

As already indicated, a new face was a significant event in the structure of Tarkovsky's films, especially if it reappeared a second time and brought to a subsequent film not only its intrinsic qualities, but also some associations. Erland Josephson, even though here playing a respectable gentleman, still trails behind him from *Nostalgia* the cloak of victim, ready to take upon himself the sins of the world.

And so this first scene links, in a schematic triangle, the three main heroes of the film's 'subject', if not of its plot: Little Man, the father and Otto. Also important in the introduction is the account Alexander gives of how they bought the house where Little Man was born and where they now live. The 'home' theme is introduced very gradually, at first only in words during that static sequence of empty landscape and the tree under which father and son are sitting. Later when Alexander is leafing through the book of icons we see the inside of the house, a well-ordered, comfortable and elegantly furnished dwelling, a real family home. It is only later, when Otto appears coming across the fields with his bulky birthday present, that we see the outside of the house for the first time, a graceful wooden house so unlike and yet so like all the family homes in Tarkovsky's work.

Home is very important – we could even say the very foundation – in the structure of Tarkovsky's world. Home is the embodiment of his eternal themes: heritage, the family and the changing generations. The idea of 'one's father's house' is one which Tarkovsky treats literally: it has to be a real house, a 'house with its windows on to the field', and not, for instance, a flat, like the city flat in *Mirror*, papered with newspapers during redecoration, or the wretched dwelling of the Stalker beside the railway yard, for both of these lack that which is essential: a house, however poor, is rich through its association with its environment, with the grass, the trees and the elements, such as cloudbursts or even conflagrations. It is just as much a part of nature as the life of the human spirit and, in a way, it is the point of contact between these.

All this is preliminary, like a preamble to the story proper, and announced without anything being especially accentuated in the introductory sequences of the film, which are constructed with a striking quality of transparency and lightness, with a minimum of camera movement and in that measured, stately rhythm which always surprises Western audiences, even those consisting of devout Tarkovsky admirers.

Captured time? Or a strange world, pregnant with catastrophies and transformations?

At this point we are introduced to the house's interior: a spacious drawing-room with a fireplace which has doors into the kitchen and on to the veranda; a typical spiral staircase leads up to the first floor, where Little Man's room is next to Alexander's study. While we are admiring the subtle grey-mother-of-pearl and green colour scheme, dissolving light and hue into a near-monochrome unity, we also try to unravel the knot of family relationships, complicated and impenetrable as always in Tarkovsky's work.

There is Alexander's English wife Adelaide (Susan Fleetwood), no doubt once beautiful, as dissatisfied as the Italian Eugenia and wearing the same type of flowing dresses (in spite of the differences in age, position and nationality, these demanding women are in some subtle

FROM SERMON TO SACRIFICE (*The Sacrifice*)

way similar), and Martha, her grown-up daughter from a previous marriage (Filippa Frantzén); then there is Victor, a doctor and a friend of the family (Sven Wollter), and we see, according to their leisured way of life, tea (or perhaps coffee) taken in the open air, where a vague rivalry emerges between mother and daughter so far as the handsome doctor is concerned. All this creates an atmosphere reminiscent of old Chekhov productions (especially since the costumes do not anchor the film in any exact time) – or rather some post-Chekhov play, for instance, Surguchev's *Autumn Violins*. There is the same kind of carefree way of life, prosperous now but soon to be nudged by history to the very edge of the precipice (*Autumn Violins* was produced by the Moscow Arts Theatre in 1914 on the eve of the First World War).

And as always in Tarkovsky, all these family frictions, this knot of 'reciprocal pain, mishaps and hurts' which could give shape to a plot, come in fact to no fruition but are pushed to the periphery by the subject of a spiritual search.

The Sacrifice has no Zone, no journey, no external peg upon which to hang this inner movement. Yet, we are given a pointer in the introduction, in the apocalyptic frame of mind we find Alexander, and another in the somewhat incongruous appearance of the postman at the family celebration. In formal terms, Otto's 'foreignness' is expressed in a tiny detail of his clothing: he is wearing black sandals and shining-white socks which make a striking intrusion on the grey-green harmony of everything else in the frame. Conversationally, Otto shocks the rationalists whose home he is in with his tales of events which are 'inexplicable, but true'.

'Inexplicable, but true' is a formulation which might be used to describe Tarkovsky's relations not with the world of science fiction, to which he was indifferent, but with the double world, the 'double being' of which Tyutchev wrote and which exists, in potential form, in all his films.

But the figure of Otto, a character not without his comic aspects (in so far as anything can be said to be comic in Tarkovsky's work, to which humour was mostly alien) is an example of just such a character from the 'boundary' world. Half-way through the conversation he suddenly falls to the floor, causing general consternation: 'An evil angel touched me with its wing' is Otto's explanation.

We should note the images juxtaposed in the editing at this point: first, the close-up of his astonished face and the fuss in the room all round him, and then we cut to the maid, Maria, whom Adelaide has allowed to go, making her way home by the flat sea-shore.

Both the servants in the house, the older Maria (Gudrun Gísladóttir) and the younger Julia (Valerie Mairesse), are placed in opposition to Adelaide, not only because they work, but because, like the women praying in the chapel of the Madonna del Parto, they represent not egoism, but giving; they are sorry for Little Man and even for Alexander himself and are ready to defend them from the caprices – some of which are, perhaps, imagined – of Madame Adelaide.

Maria (we remember that Gorchakov's wife was also Maria) has a very special part to play in the film. Julia, too, is no stranger to odd events in Alexander's house – when a crescendo of sound fills the room, the glass in her hand begins to vibrate, the beads tinkle in the chandelier and a jug of milk suddenly lurches and falls.

Since *Solaris*, the director and his regular composer Eduard Artemiev had learned to use sound as a means to convey this sense of the 'inexplicable, but true'. It was sound, rather than the few less than successful images of it, that conveyed the life of the conscious Ocean on Solaris. In the same way, it was the film's soundtrack with its cracking, bells, whistles and distant bird-song, curdling together into a kind of pre-musical harmony, which created the particular atmosphere that signified the Zone in *Stalker*. But just as Tarkovsky had idea-faces and emblem-images as signposts to what is happening, he also has sound-pointers, including the crescendo of rattle and whine which causes the trembling, tinkling and displacement of fragile glass things – whether it be the rumble of passing trains, as in *Stalker*, the thunder of a low-flying aeroplane, as in *Nostalgia*, or a wail like a bomb being detonated overhead, as in *The Sacrifice*. In the 'captured time' of the film it heralds 'inexplicable, but true' changes.

Now we see an enormous Alexander, filling the frame as he leans over his tiny house. In fact, he has happened upon the birthday surprise prepared for him by his son – which does not, of course, prevent him in the composition of the frame from seeming something like a giant. Little Man's room, with yet another metal bed-head (although this time, a graceful one) against the background of a whitewashed wall, is the central focus of this house and of all Alexander's thoughts. There is nothing strange in the fact that the irruption of the 'other form of reality' into an ordinary birthday, signalled by the sound from the boundary world, should again be signposted by a zoom into the Epiphany, which also has the status of an emblem within the stucture of the film. For at this point Otto and Alexander, heads close together, are staring point-blank into the glass of the reproduction.

And from this moment begins Alexander's actual dream.

Those who would wish to approach the film with the yardstick of common sense will of course consider Alexander's efforts to save the world single-handed somewhat laughable and even mad (Domenico, in *Nostalgia*, was also considered mad by all around him). What, we may well ask, is *The Sacrifice* – an apocalyptic dream, or an episode in the life of a madman? Of course, it is partly a dream, and the transition is signalled with that subtle but consistent logic that is the mark of these things in Tarkovsky's work: the sound is the overture, and the peering into the Leonardo reproduction, as into a mirror, is the beginning of the dream. But from what happens in his dream, Alexander will draw his own conclusions upon awaking, and in them he will be no madder than, say, Hamlet or Ivan Karamazov, for his bad dreams are not a metaphor: no, they are rather a paraphrase of general reality, expressed in terms of his own personal life. Like all Tarkovsky's films, and more than any of the others, *The Sacrifice* is both specific and symbolic at one and the same time.

In the screenplay we can see more nakedly expressed than in the final film the director's own personal circumstances: illness striking, a fear of death that was in no way purely academic, the suffering caused by his concern for his son, to whom 'in hope and faith' Tarkovsky dedicated his film. These personal circumstances, however, changed nothing in the overall direction of his work, in the inexorable inner imperative it had always followed.

Alexander's dream is clothed in forms that are perfectly realistic: as always, apart from the 'Icarus complex'[2] and the dystopic devastation (which we have since seen in *Letters from a Dead Man*[3]), it seems outwardly like any other family drama. But the modality is unreal, that of 'how it could have been, if . . .'

Alexander changes the station on his radio, which had been playing some creaking, scratchy music, and hears the announcement that the country is at war. He goes downstairs. In the bluish, flickering light of the television screen the camera pans slowly over the faces, each one looking so pale, and comes to rest on Josephson's in close-up. To the postman's tactless earlier remark of which we have already spoken, he now has the answer: 'I've been waiting for this all my life.'

The television flickers and dies. The play of light and shade is succeeded by hysterics from the wife, and now it is her silken legs which suddenly flash naked before us. Together with her female terrors, her hidden passions, too, are nakedly revealed: her attachment to the doctor, her veiled rivalry with her daughter. The doctor gives her a sedative injection, and Julia, the maid, resists her intention to awaken Little Man: 'Don't scare him! I won't allow him to be tormented!' Among these family squabbles, the camera moves in once again on the Leonardo reproduction, showing us that something important is about to begin.

Alexander, unacquainted with God, as he put it to Otto, addresses him in prayer for the first time in his life. He prays for his family, whatever the relations between whichever of its members, for Little Man, 'for this war is the last war, the terrible war after which there will remain neither victors nor vanquished, neither towns nor villages, neither grass nor trees, neither water in the springs nor birds in the firmament', and he promises to renounce everything, his home, his family, Little Man, and to give up speech itself, if only all can be as it had been before. It is, of course, a madman's prayer, an invocation, like the Stalker's hope, that only a truly wretched listener could understand. At this moment of evil for him, Alexander is shown, as always with Tarkovsky, in the most prosaic light possible: he crawls to his couch almost on all fours. And again the hallucinations surge in, a dream within the dream, with the same crescendo of sound, with rubbish and mud and then finally snow underfoot. Again we zoom in

FROM SERMON TO SACRIFICE (*The Sacrifice*)

on the Epiphany, as though to introduce yet another spiral in the terrible dream, the conversation with Otto. This decisive conversation, visually, is no less silly than it sounds: Alexander is wrapped in a woman's shawl, Otto's socks are bright blobs of white in the light of the paraffin lamp (the electricity has been cut off), and they sit whispering on the floor like two madmen. What Otto proposes to Alexander seems even more ridiculous than what has previously happened on this ridiculous day: he must get out the bicycle, ride to the farm where Maria, the maid, lives, and sleep with her. This is the only way to save the world. We are reminded of Piero della Francesca as a counterweight to Leonardo, the Piero della Francesca who painted the Madonna del Parto.

The mythological meaning of this strange idea will become a little clearer if we remember the sequence where Alexander, enormous in close-up, is looking down like a giant at the tiny house and at the same time talking to Maria. Strangely enough, he obeys Otto, and taking a revolver from the doctor's bag he leaves the house in the blue half-light, clambers on to Otto's broken bicycle (not without falling into a puddle on the way) and sets off along the road to the farm.

The scene at Maria's is depicted with Tarkovsky's usual mundane and prosaic realism, that is to say with the realistic absurdity of an unromantic man, no longer young and certainly far from convinced of his messianic mission, trying to explain to the maid why she should get into bed with him; but at the same time it is suffused with a symbolism that has both a mythological and a Christian power.

When Alexander dismounts at Maria's door, he has to wait for a flock of sheep to pour across the road in his path. Sheep are normal domestic animals which graze on these flat, coastal plains; but somewhere in our minds lurks the idea of a saving victim, of the Lamb of God. Alexander tells Maria about his mother's illness and about her neglected garden which he mutilated, imagining that he was making it beautiful for her. If he was the god of that garden, it was a case of pillage rather than creation. Finally, with a revolver to his temple, Alexander finally begs for Maria to show him her love or her mercy, and the sharing of that mercy causes them to float weightless (as in *Solaris* and in *Mirror*) above the snow-white sheets of Maria's bed.

Among all these mythological signifiers – all, of course, open to different interpretations – there are also pointers from Tarkovsky's own code: the same boundary sound from the other reality, for instance, which quickens inanimate objects into movement and brings about ascensions. Then: 'the bright, bright day', a redundant light-bulb shining brightly, the Leonardo reproduction hanging over the couch, and Alexander waking from his deep and terrible dream.

A dream? The director gives the audience two, apparently contradictory hints. On the one hand, a call to the newspaper convinces Alexander that nothing has happened in the external world, that everything he experienced has taken place within his inner self. On the other hand, there is a pain in the leg he hurt when he fell off the bicycle in the night. But, after all, the leg was hurt in that inner world, the one that parallels this outer world of ours, and Alexander is limping badly, even though the external emblem of the boundary between the two, the Epiphany – which in the light of day has lost some of its sinister power – has separated the 'real' modality of atomic war from the reality of morning in the Alexander household. The table is laid outside for breakfast on the lawn: all this is filmed in a way that is so translucent, so clear in the diffused northern light. The conversation, as always, is of such little substance (the doctor is intending to go to Australia, while no one wants to let him leave) and seems so ordinary that Alexander's nocturnal revelations seem submerged by this picture of a typically peaceful morning.

So we come to the film's epilogue, as leisurely as was the introduction, although the ambiguous figure of Otto the postman has now melted away. The events of this epilogue could indeed be termed Alexander's 'sacrifice', for he takes both his prayer (even if it did take place during his dream) and his promise completely seriously. Having robed himself in his dressing-gown with the Tao Yin-and-Yang symbol on the back, he sends everyone off for a walk by means of a note, and piles all the furniture up on the veranda with ritual fervour for a final *auto-da-fé*.

To carry the flame through the water – that was what mad Domenico demanded of Andrey – Domenico was prepared to become the flame himself, to be the burning bush we first heard mentioned as

FROM SERMON TO SACRIFICE (*The Sacrifice*)

far back as *Mirror*. Alexander consigns to the flames all his worldly possessions. And so flares up the last of Tarkovsky's conflagrations, like a demonstration of the power of Nature – or perhaps like a pillar of fire, or a fire of sacrifice, a consuming fire. Alexander proceeds through the waters of the puddles, each one transformed into a slim stratum of earthly firmament. Everyone else chases after him, splashing through the sheets of water beneath their feet, while he pretends to attempt escape from the orderlies in white jackets who jump out of a white ambulance, having appeared from nowhere; then he kisses the hand of Maria the maid and slams the door of the ambulance shut behind him, all this without a word because he has taken a vow of silence. Adelaide, exhausted, sinks down into a puddle.

And now, just as we saw in *Ivan's Childhood*, *Andrey Rublyov*, *Solaris*, *Mirror*, and later in *Stalker* and *Nostalgia*, after this protracted, absurd and exalted finale, with the inexorability of the 'dynamic stereotype', there follows the true epilogue. To the solemn rhythms of Bach the white ambulance moves away, down the road of life, and beneath the dead tree (which he has just watered, as ordered in the parable) lies Little Man. 'In the beginning was the Word. Why Papa?' he suddenly asks, as though Alexander's own vow of silence has suddenly loosened the sound in his son. Then the camera pans slowly up the length of the dead tree, and through the stumps of the branches we see the sky and the flat sea, depth and distance and height. 'The effort of resurrection', which was the driving force in all Tarkovsky's films, has been achieved in *The Sacrifice*.

Epilogue : After the Retrospective

I never dreamed that I would be attending a Tarkovsky Memorial Retrospective in Moscow, but all the films, including *The Sacrifice*, were shown in the spring of 1987 at Dom Kino, the headquarters of the Film-Makers' Union. The occasion was a moving one.

It seems like only yesterday that he burst upon the scene with a power and vigour matched only by the abruptness of his end. Seven and a half films: it does not seem much when you add them up, but within these he created a whole world.

The retrospective showed Tarkovsky's development through time, proving the oneness of the world – a single entity, and not simply the sum of its separate parts. Their length seemed compressed into the next film, making it a larger step along the way, no doubt because of Tarkovsky's constant awareness of the duty to labour on, as the poet puts it, 'day and night, day and night'. That is probably also the reason why he was prickly and uncomfortable to work with, often irritable, and accutely contrary by nature; but in defending the honour of his art he was straightforward, open, and completely fearless. He could only do *his* work, in *his* way, and never agreed to anything else.

This uncompromising quality is there in the films, as well; they are separate, different, and distinctive, which is perhaps why they have not dated in our fast-moving age. They are *interesting*, in some sense even more so now than when they were shocking in their novelty, when they seemed 'difficult' or even 'contentious' pictures. Now that the novelty has been assimilated into the history of cinema, both the personal and the universal are easier to discern.

EPILOGUE : AFTER THE RETROSPECTIVE

Even his diploma film, the unpretentious short *The Steamroller and the Violin*, feels now like an animated portrait of the times, the end of the fifties, and all the hopes they offered before the gates clanged shut again.

This was, in every sense, a *young* film, and it was also perfectly natural that in *Ivan's Childhood* (a film which marked a radical new departure in 1962 and in which we can almost hear the wheels of history turning), the stitching should still show in places – be it in the make-up or in the lighting – to a degree which is almost touching; after all, this film marks a change not only of cinematic style, but of times and attitudes as well. Something else, however, does strike us as extraordinary – the continuity of meaning and the way we instantly recognize the hand behind the film. Something which we had thought of as integral to the subject matter turned out to be integral to the director himself. In this, his first full-length film, Tarkovsky had defined himself, and now we can see with hindsight that it was this epiphany of a new young director that caused such a stir at that historic Venice Film Festival. Tarkovsky was lucky to emerge in his own time, but also at a time when the world looked towards cinema with bated breath. It was a lucky coincidence, and in the light of it the distance between his sensational debut and the classical cadences of *Andrey Rublyov* seems all the more enormous.

In this, the 'archetypal' costume drama, we are blissfully unaware of either costumes or make-up. The fifteenth century is so thoroughly absorbed that we feel as much at home in it as in our daily lives, although 'daily life' figures no more in *Rublyov* than it does in any of Tarkovsky's other films. It is not that they are trying to be 'above' the details of daily life, or to ignore them; daily life is simply something in parallel, to the side, that does not impinge upon the 'captured time' of Tarkovsky's films, which ideally, according to his theory, should be the *whole* of time, with nothing left excluded.

A stormy birth brought forth a classic film, as the director was well aware; he also knew that what happened to the film would happen to many more that he was yet to make, although none of his films suffered for as long as that of his co-author, Andrey Mikhalkov-Konchalovsky, whose *Asya's Happiness* saw light of day only in 1987.

The years that *Rublyov* lay on the shelf, putting physical and emotional constraints on its author, just as his talent was coming into its own, must have had a profound effect upon Tarkovsky, whose spirit was ill-suited to displays of patience, to compromise or (especially) to sitting idle.

Strangely enough *Solaris*, which when first shown in Europe seemed a significant, but self-indulgently over-long film, is now revealed in context as a tightly constructed and well-thought-out picture. It is *not* science fiction, which its author so disliked and tried to negate 'from within', but a separate genre. 'Parable' is perhaps too strong a word; better, perhaps, to call it an instructive exploration of human behaviour seen in a context which has elements borrowed from the world of science fiction. Once Tarkovsky had discovered the realm, he was to make it his own throughout the rest of his short life. What strikes us now in this film is the wealth of a complex hierarchy of motifs (which in later years he would strive to simplify) and the sheer richness of puslating vitality it displays. We now know that this richness was due, in part, to the fact that its subject matter, from a world completely external to that of the director, had absorbed much from the autobiographical film which he was beginning to conceive at the same time and that was later to become *Mirror*.

Mirror is the fixed point at the centre of Tarkovsky's entire creation. There he succeeded in something that few can achieve: giving life to the world of his childhood, recreating his home, peopling his memories, and capturing time itself. What happened to *Mirror*, neither banned nor completely permitted – as Chekhov would have put it – was no less dramatic and no doubt just as traumatic as the five-year classification of *Andrey Rublyov* as a 'non-film'. Most important, it was a step towards self-knowledge and self-determination in both social and human terms that struck an immediate chord for a whole generation. As Arseniy Tarkovsky put it:

> There is nothing on the earth
> That I would find dearer
> Than the lilting babbling
> Of my childhood memories.

EPILOGUE : AFTER THE RETROSPECTIVE

In a paradoxical way this most plotless and subjective of films, which did not even seek to be understood, was the one which brought Tarkovsky his first awareness of interconnection with his public, an interaction which echoed his quickening sense of communication with the past, with the life of his family and his birthright.

After the breadth and ambition of *Andrey Rublyov*, *Solaris* and *Mirror*, *Stalker* strikes us as ascetic, yet strictly structured, in a new way, as if it were the crystallization of the new genre Tarkovsky had discovered. The observation of the classical unities gives it a purposeful tautness of plot, sound and vision. This consistency of plot is not, however, the reason why the word 'problematical' was for once not applied to one of Tarkovsky's films, since little had changed in his manner of working. What had changed were the times, and the audiences: a new television generation, for whom a visual language was something perfectly natural and normal, and for whom Tarkovsky's work was not a puzzle to be solved but a dialogue between equals, one of whom was albeit a very demanding equal. Understanding was achieved, but – as so often – it had come too late.

The broadening of his geographical surroundings became for Tarkovsky a new step in the direction of self-knowledge. He had tackled the theme of his family home by distancing himself from it through time and the prism of maturity; and he became aware of a homesickness for the country of his birth when he went forth and met a different culture. Really to know something you have to go beyond it, though knowledge and expression, in the form of some statement, were not Tarkovsky's immediate objectives.

If *Stalker* had captured a moment of apocalyptic despair – a despair which engulfs so many artists in these disjointed times – then the discordant and tormented *Nostalgia* is an attempt to get through to those who would hear, even at the price of life itself.

Nobody will ever know what the relationship was between Tarkovsky's talent and the disease which was eating him away. I have always believed that the body knows more about itself than the mind does, and that though Nature is often kind enough to hide from the mind what is happening, the blind knowledge of the body is a powerful creative stimulant for a personality such as Tarkovsky's. It could well be that his homesickness also aggravated his illness. By the time he filmed *The Sacrifice*, Tarkovsky knew that he was ill and knew what he had, even having to interrupt the filming for spells in hospital. In spite of this, or perhaps even because of it, *The Sacrifice* is one of the most translucent of all his films.

This film is something of a fresco in its unity, its colours, its lapidary quality in spite of the complexities of structure. It summarizes the main motifs of Tarkovsky's life in art. It does not flinch from openly expressing a moral message (for Tarkovsky, 'freedom' means first and foremost the freedom to sacrifice oneself). For its author, *The Sacrifice* was more than the telling of a story, however well constructed; more than a moral impulse, and even more than a last will and testament. For him this film was an exorcism, a gauntlet flung down to fate, an act of magic, an emanation of his artistic will to act upon reality and change it, change it by becoming a part of it and entering the world on fully equal terms.

This is one of the rarest gifts of all in our day, this faith in art not simply as a social, logical or aesthetic concept but as reality and action, as a direct force in life.

Maybe it was this that hid the secret of Tarkovsky's ceaseless embodiment of his own inner core in film, whatever his external circumstances and inconsistencies, and the secret of the stability of that Tarkovsky world that seemed to exist even before any of the films. As Arseniy Tarkovsky wrote:

> It may be idiocy
> To pay, in full, your life
> For the fact of resemblance
> Between the poems and the man.[1]

Notes

Introduction

1 Boris Pasternak, 'In all my ways' (c. 1958), from *In the Interlude: Poems 1945–60*, translated by Henry Kamen, Oxford University Press, 1962, p. 53.
2 Robert Bresson, *Notes on Cinematography*, translated by Jonathan Griffin, Urizen Press, New York, 1977, p. 39.
3 An edited transcript of the *Guardian* Lecture was published as 'Against Interpretation: an interview with Andrei Tarkovsky' in *Framework*, No. 14, London 1981; see p. 48 (all other quotations otherwise unattributed from this interview).
4 Thus a March 1983 *Pravda* article acknowledged that there would be conflicts even in a socialist society and stated that when things are wrong the artist is one of the physicians who can help heal society. But in May 1984, under Chernenko, a Central Committee resolution roundly condemned films which 'idealize outmoded moral norms', and criticized the bulk of production as 'weak and uninteresting' and lacking 'positive Communist heroes'.
5 See my report on Klimov's election as First Secretary of the Film-Makers' Union, '*Perestroika* in Person', *Sight and Sound*, Vol. 56, No. 3, Summer 1978, p. 156; also William Fisher, 'Gorbachev's Cinema', *Sight and Sound*, Vol. 56, No. 4, Autumn 1987, pp. 238–43. On the impact of the 1928–30 'cultural revolution', see R. Taylor and I. Christie, eds, *The Film Factory: Russian and Soviet Cinema in Documents 1896–1939*, Routledge/Harvard University Press, 1988, pp. 191 *et seq*.
6 Mikhail Romm's (1901–71) films cited are: *Lenin in October* (1937), *Lenin in 1918* (1938), *The Russian Question* (1948), *Nine Days of One Year* (1962) and *Ordinary Fascism* (1965).
7 Stan Brakhage records an encounter with Tarkovsky at the 1983 Telluride Festival, when the latter 'lashed out in a diatribe against innovation itself . . . "What I say is that innovation is reckless and destructive." ' *Rolling Stock*, No. 6, Colorado, 1983, p. 13.
8 Erwin Panofsky, 'Style and Medium in the Motion Picture', in *Film: An Anthology*, ed. Daniel Talbot, University of California Press 1966, p. 30 (article first published 1934).

9 See p. 18. *The Great Warrior Skanderbeg* (1954), a Soviet-Albanian co-production, directed by Sergey Yutkevich.
10 *Sculpting in Time*, Faber, 1989, pp. 79–80.
11 W. H. Auden, 'Musée des Beaux Arts', *Collected Shorter Poems 1930–44*, Faber, 1960.
12 See my 'Raising the Shroud', *Monthly Film Bulletin*, February 1987, pp. 37–8; and 'Eisenstein at 90', *Sight and Sound*, Vol. 57, No. 3, Summer 1988, pp. 181–8.
13 Naum Kleiman, curator of the Eisenstein Museum in Moscow, was a contemporary of Tarkovsky at VGIK and remembers the impact *Ivan* Part 2 had on the young Tarkovsky.
14 *Sculpting in Time*, p. 68.
15 An interesting review of *Sculpting in Time* in the *Times Literary Supplement* (9 January 1987) by the Russian émigré writer Zinovy Zinik sees Tarkovsky as a traditional Russian and Soviet intellectual, fearful of ideological and political involvement, and suspicious of Western civilization – hence his cherished belief in 'inner freedom' and spirituality.
16 *Sculpting in Time*, pp. 117–21.
17 André Bazin, 'The Ontology of the Photographic Image', in *What is Cinema?*, ed. and translator Hugh Gray, University of California Press, 1967, pp. 14–15.
18 Michelangelo's Sonnet lxxxiii, quoted in Anthony Blunt, *Artistic Theory in Italy 1450–1600*, Oxford 1940, p. 73.
19 *Sculpting in Time*, pp. 63–4.
20 See Michel Chion, 'La Maison où il pleut: sur l'esthétique de Tarkovski', *Cahiers du cinéma*, No. 358, April 1984.
21 See, for instance, Peter Nichols's report on Tarkovsky's 'defection' (*The Times*, 10 July 1984), claiming that *The Hunter* (i.e. *Stalker*) had 'never been shown in the Soviet Union'; while in an interview with Angus MacKinnon in *Time Out* (9–15 August 1984), Tarkovsky referred to *Komsomolskaya Pravda* stating that *Stalker* had been 'one of the USSR's six most commercially successful films'.
22 Clarence Brown, *Mandelstam*, Cambridge University Press, 1973, pp. 231–2.

Prologue

1 *Literaturnaya gazeta* is an influential journal, the official organ of the Soviet Writers' Union, which ranges far beyond literature and the arts.
2 An English translation of Vladimir Bogomolov's novella, by Bernard Isaacs, was published by Raduga (Moscow) in 1987.
3 21 June 1941 was the date of the German invasion of the Soviet Union, which broke the non-aggression pact agreed between Stalin and Hitler in 1939.
4 These references are to: Sergei Urusevsky, influntial lighting cameraman on *The Cranes Are Flying* (1957) and other films directed by Kalatozov; Mikhail Sholokov's four-part novel sequence *Quiet Flows the Don* (1928–40); *The Lay of Igor's Campaign*, a celebrated medieval Russian poem in which Igor fatefully

ignores the bad omen of a solar eclipse; and, in the following quotation, Aleksandr Blok (1880–1921), the symbolist poet and playwright who lent his support to the October Revolution.
5 A reference perhaps to one of the popular classics of Soviet cinema, Barnet's *Exploits of an Intelligence Agent* (1947), an exciting tale of clandestine operations behind enemy lines which is still regularly revived on television.
6 'Dynamic stereotype' was a term used by Pavlov in his research on 'habitual reflexes'. See *Collected Works*, Moscow–Leningrad, 1951, Vol. III, Bk. 2, p. 240.
7 'Poetry and Prose in the Cinema', first published in *Poetika kino*, ed. Boris Eikhenbaum, Moscow, 1927.
8 English translation in *The Film Factory*, p. 178.

Chapter 1

1 Second poem from the cycle *The Student*: 'There is an hour, a burden now thrown off.'
2 Some of the names and films that emerged while Tarkovsky and his contemporaries were going through their formative period are: in 1954, Josif Heifits' *The Great Family*, bearing early and timid, but nonetheless significant, witness to this shift in the cinema world; in 1956 the début of a whole constellation of young directors, cameramen, screen-writers, actors – those who have now become the elder, but not the eldest, generation in the cinema.
    Over those two years – 1955–6 – no fewer than fifty films were made by young directors. Among them were:
    - *A Man is Born* (Ordynsky, screenplay by Agranovich)
    - *Strangers in the Family* (Shveitser, story by Tendryakov, starring Mordiukova and Rybnikov)
    - *Earth and Men* (Rostotsky, based on Troyepolsky's village scenes)
    - *Hop, Skip and a Jump* (Samsonov, based on Chekhov's story, starring Sergey Bondarchuk as Dr Dymov)
    - *Carnival Night* (Ryazanov, starring Igor Ilinsky and the young Ludmilla Gurchenko)
    - *The Forty-First* (Chukhrai, based on Lavryonov's story)
    - *Pavel Korchagin* (Alov and Naumov)
    - *Magdana's Donkey* (Abuladze and Chkheidze)
    - *Spring on Zarachnaya Street* (Khutsiev and Mironer).
3 Andrey Mikhalkov-Konchalovsky (born 1937), half-brother of the actor and film director Nikita Mikhalkov. His second film as a director, *Asya's Happiness*, was 'shelved' in 1967 and not released until 1987–8. He left the USSR to work abroad in the early eighties and began a prolific English-language career as Andrey Konchalovsky with *Maria's Lovers* in 1985.
4 *The Dream*, although written in 1939–40 and largely shot in 1941 before the German invasion, was not released until 1943.

Chapter 2

1 *Chapayev* (1934) became not only a touchstone of 'socialist realism', but also the first popular success of Soviet sound cinema.

Chapter 3

1 The production personnel at Mosfilm at this time were divided into so-called 'Creative Units', each headed by a well-known director. To all intents and purposes, the 'unit' functioned for the individual director as a producer would in the West.
2 The war was to remain Bogomolov's favourite subject, and fifteen years later he would again attract attention as the author of the well-known *In August '44 . . .*, a novel about the workings of the anti-espionage organization SMERSH, which in spite of its excellent qualities has not yet been adapted for the screen. This is not because the cinema does not know a good thing when it sees it: on the contrary, the author was immediately asked to provide a screenplay. But all attempts by directors to meddle with the complex, many-layered, 'alienated' structure of the novel have foundered on its author's intransigence. He preferred to do without the fame which a screen version of his book can bring to a young author and without the money that comes in its wake, stopping the film when it was already in production rather than see distorted his vision of war as work which requires a highly professional dedication. The interesting thing is that although it might be fanciful to discern in the montage structure of the novel the direct influence of the film *Ivan's Childhood*, there is definitely a cinematic quality about it.

Chapter 4

1 Andrey Voznesensky (born 1933) first attracted attention with the poems 'Master Craftsman' and 'Goya' in 1958–9, before he was denounced by Khrushchev in 1963 as a 'bourgeois formalist'.
2 *La Dolce Vita* was released in the USSR during the 'thaw' and contributed to Fellini's great popularity and influence.
3 Siegfried Kracauer's *The Nature of Film* (1960) is subtitled 'The Redemption of Physical Reality'. An abridged Russian translation was published in 1974.
4 Sergo Ordzhonikidze, a close associate of Stalin in the early twenties who was censured by Lenin for his violence, played a vital part in the first Five Year Plans as commissar for heavy industry.
5 This image of the revolutionary saint, the frenzied zealot, was given a tragic, poetic, polemical treatment by Tarkovsky's older colleagues Alov and Naumov in the character of Pavel Korchagin, the hero of Nikolay Ostrovsky's famous autobiographical novel *How The Steel Was Tempered*, which they filmed in 1956

under the title *Pavel Korchagin*. The novel was also filmed by Donskoy in 1942 (I.C.).
6 In 1963 the screenplay was transferred from Mosfilm's First Creative Unit to the Sixth, where Tarkovsky would also make *Mirror*.
7 The 'literary script' of a Soviet film is often published considerably in advance of its production in one of several specialized journals. This may differ substantially from the resulting film – and in some cases the published script has stood as a monument to a 'shelved' or unmade film. (I.C.).

Chapter 5

1 Stanislaw Lem (born 1921), Polish writer who began publishing optimistic 'socialist realist' science fiction in the fifties before turning to the satirical and speculative works for which he is internationally famous. These include *Solaris* (1971) and *The Invincible* (1973).
2 I too played my part in the disputes about *Solaris*:
Ecology, a word which we never used to hear before, has become not simply fashionable, but the expression of an intense human need. The water, air, grass and foliage about which we never stopped to think before, just as a traveller does not notice the humble plantain growing by the path, are suddenly revealed to be fragile and vulnerable; and now that our Earth has been seen from the outside, from Space, it seems shrunk like a childhood home revisited years later in adulthood. Suddenly the Earth has earned the right to that heart-wrenching love which Tarkovsky has called 'the saving bitterness of nostalgia'.
3 In Russian 'nostalgia' denotes a longing for home rather than for the past. (I.C.).

Chapter 6

1 In the decade of *cinéma vérité*, both television and cinema made extensive use of candid interview formats, as in Rouch and Morin's *Chronicle of a Summer* (France, 1962). A Soviet equivalent, Khutsiev's *I Am Twenty*, provoked Khrushchev's wrath and suffered extensive revision.
2 At the same time I and my fellow script-writer, Yury Khaniutin, put to Mikhail Romm, with whom we had worked on *Ordinary Fascism*, the idea of making a film about an apparently unmotivated murder. We found ourselves a current case, and proposed exactly the same thing: filming in the courtroom with hidden cameras and filling out this record by interviewing the defendants, the mothers of the victim and the killer, neighbours and witnesses. We even proposed using actors to show the killing through the eyes of the various characters, together with contemporary archive material. Unfortunately, Romm was busy at the time with the idea of a film about the future of the world (*And*

Nonetheless I Believe) on which his students were working, and we did not wish for the documentary sequences to be replaced by staged ones. So, all that came of the idea was a script, published in part in the January 1967 issue of *The Journalist* under the title 'No Mitigating Circumstances'.
Of course, Tarkovsky knew nothing about our ideas nor we about his.
And Nonetheless I Believe was completed in 1973, after Romm's death, by Khutsiev and Klimov (I.C.).

3 'Discours sur le plan-séquence où le cinéma comme sémiologie de la réalité', *Cahiers du cinéma*, Paris, 1967, No. 192, p. 28.
This sequence was partly anticipated by the demolition sequence in *The Steamroller and the Violin* and partly by the image of the roofless church in *Ivan's Childhood*.

5 This sequence was even written separately by Tarkovsky and published as a memoir in *Iskusstvo kino*.

6 Fedor Tyutchev (1803–73) metaphysical poet; the greatest Russian poet of the nineteenth century after Pushkin, whose reputation was revived by the Symbolists.

7 Tarkovsky's mother – Maria Ivanovna Vishnyakova – was a proofreader at the Model Printing Press No. 1 and worked there until the day she retired.

Chapter 7

1 Osip Mandelstam, *Octet VII*, 'Schubert on the water and Mozart in the songbirds' scales'.
2 It is interesting to note that this was the very name given – although for quite different reasons – by Voznesensky to one of his poems.
3 *Iskusstvo kino*, No. 4, 1967, p. 78.
4 Tarkovsky collaborated with Friedrich Gorenstein on a screenplay based on Aleksandr Belyaev's *Ariel*, also titled *A Light Breeze* (*Svetly veter*), which has not been published.
Belyaev is credited with introducing the theme of biological change in humans in his science fiction of the late twenties: the heroes of *The Amphibious Man* and *Ariel* can move freely in water and air respectively (I.C.).
5 Snow falling on a roofless church is also, of course, one of the closing images of *Nostalgia*.
6 Many historic Russian churches were destroyed during the thirties, ostensibly to make way for new buildings, but also to attack the Church's visible status. Among the most notorious demolitions were that of the Cathedral of Christ the Saviour, built by public subscription, in 1931 (its site is now a swimming pool); and the seventeenth-century monastery, blown up in 1937, which stood where the Rossiya Cinema now is. (I.C.)
7 See Sigmund Freud, *The Interpretation of Dreams*, Discus books, New York, pp. 305–7, 428–30.

8 It is interesting that this theme emerged in the work of Tarkovsky at almost exactly the same time as in the poetry of Voznesensky, who wrote: 'I am a monument to my father Andrey Nikolayevich.' The external circumstance may have been the death of Voznesensky's own father, but the motif was typical of a whole generation.
9 Nikolay Grinko (born 1920) is a well-known Soviet character actor in both theatre and cinema who has played a great variety of parts, but was always cast in a similar role by Tarkovsky.

Chapter 8

1 Joseph Brodsky, 'Odysseus to Telemachus' from *Selected Poems*, trans. George L. Kline, Penguin Books, 1973.
2 André Bazin, 'The Ontology of the Photographic Image' (first published in *Problèmes de la Peinture*, Paris, 1945; collected in *Qu'est-ce que le cinéma?*, Editions du Cerf, Paris, 1958–65). 'The cinema is objectivity in time. The film is no longer content to preserve the object, enshrouded as it were in an instant . . . The film delivers baroque art from its convulsive catalepsy. Now, for the first time, the image of things is likewise the image of their duration, change mummified . . .' English translation by Hugh Gray, *What is Cinema?*, University of California Press, 1967, pp. 14–15. A Russian translation of Bazin's writings appeared in 1972, although his ideas were already current. (I.C.)
3 *Iskusstvo kino*, 1967, No. 4, pp. 70–2.
4 *Iskusstvo kino*, 1979, No. 3, p. 92.
5 Ibid., p. 91.
6 'Chronotope', literally 'time space' was a term borrowed from mathematics and Einstein's theory of relativity by the eminent Russian literary theorist Mikhail Bakhtin (1895–1975). Borrowed for literary criticism 'almost as a metaphor', 'it expresses the inseparability of space and time (time as the fourth dimension of space) . . . In the literary artistic chronotope, spatial and temporal indicators are fused into one carefully thought-out, concrete whole. Time, as it were, thickens, takes on flesh, becomes artistically visible; likewise space becomes charged and responsive to the movements of time, plot and history. This intersection of axes and fusion of indicators characterizes the artistic chronotope.' 'Forms of time and of the Chronotope in the Novel' (first published 1975), in *The Dialogic Imagination: Four Essays by M. M. Bakhtin*, ed. Michael Holquist, translated by Caryl Emerson and Michael Holquist, University of Texas Press, 1981, p. 84. (I.C.)
7 Compilations of Second World War newsreel footage combined with the worldwide impact of Italian neo-realism and influential theories of Bazin and Kracauer to make newsreel a universal token of 'authenticity' in fiction films. (I.C.)
8 By 'the whole of time' we are, of course, referring to human time. For

Tarkovsky, neither time nor space existed outside the human dimension and its concerns.

9 French director Alexandre Astruc used this term in an article for *Écran français*, 1948, No. 144; translated as 'The Birth of a New Avant-Garde: La Caméra-Stylo', *The New Wave*, ed. Peter Graham, Secker and Warburg, 1968. It has since come to stand for the ideal of unmediated self-expression in cinema. (I.C.)
10 See Vyacheslav Ivanov, 'Even and Odd: The Asymmetry of the Brain and Semantic Systems', *Soviet Radio*, Moscow, 1978, p. 129.
11 This chapter was first written when Tarkovsky was known to be at work on the adaptation of the Strugatsky brothers' *Roadside Picnic*, which eventually became *Stalker*. He also worked on *Ariel* with Gorenstein, as already noted.

Chapter 9

1 'My Sister, Life' from *Philosophy Class: The Definition of Poetry*.
2 Bela Balazs (1884–1949) was an important early theorist of the film medium, whose *Der sichtbare Mensch, oder Die Kultur des Films* (*The Visible Man, or Film Culture*), 1924, argued that cinema would restore 'the subtler means of expression provided by the body' after an era dominated by the printed word. Now, 'Man has again become visible'. And film would constitute a new visual language in its own right, eventually making 'the inner man' visible. See Balazs, *Theory of the Film*, Denis Dobson, London, 1970, pp. 39–45 (summarizing *Der sichtbare Mensch*). (I.C.)
3 See Ivanov, op. cit., p. 39.
4 *Sculpting in Time*, p. 120.
5 Innokenty Annensky has a sonnet called 'The Changing Pulse of Rhythm'.
6 Shklovsky, op. cit. (Prologue, no. 8), pp. 176–7.

Chapter 10

1 At this time there were six Creative Units functioning as autonomous production groups within Mosfilm Studios.
2 Arkady (born 1925) and Boris (born 1933) Strugatsky have been leading Soviet science-fiction writers since the late fifties. Among their other translated works are: *Hard to Be a God* (1964), *A Snail on the Slope* (1968) and *A Billion Years Before the End of the World* (1978).
3 Aleksandr Kaidanovsky (born 1946) worked as an actor in the theatre between 1969–72 and in the cinema from 1969. He has emerged in recent years as a director of such striking experimental films as *The Garden* (1983), *Iona* (1984), *A Simple Death* (1985), *The Guest* (1988), and *The Kerosene Seller's Wife* (1989). (I.C.)

4 The article from which this extract comes appeared in a highly independent journal *Kino*, published in Riga, 1980, No. 6, pp. 2–5.
5 There are many examples of Christian symbolism in recent Soviet films, such as Lopushansky's *Letters from a Dead Man* and Abuladze's *Repentance*, which ends with the line: 'What is the good of a road which does not lead to a church?' (I.C.)
6 'Art is Created by People: Conversation with AT after the Tallin Première of *Stalker*', *Kino*, Riga, 1979, No. 11, pp. 20–2.
7 The name Chernobyl, where the nuclear disaster occurred, evoked for many Russian Christians the prediction in the Apocalypse that a 'star named Wormwood' would fall to earth and lay waste much of it. So great was the concern that the Archbishop of Kiev wrote in *Literaturnaya gazeta* to deny any link. (I.C.)

Chapter 11

1 *Sculpting in Time*, pp. 192–3.
2 Tonino Guerra (born 1920), Italian scriptwriter and frequent collaborator with such directors as Fellini, Antonioni, and Angelopoulos. He was married to a Russian.
3 Erland Josephson (born 1923), Swedish stage and film actor, and latterly director. Best known abroad for his roles in later Ingmar Bergman films such as *Scenes from a Marriage* and *Fanny and Alexander*.
4 *Sculpting in Time*, pp. 147–8.

Chapter 12

1 Sergey Bondarchuck, a leading conservative from the Soviet film establishment, was on the 1984 Cannes jury and is reliably reported to have fought against *Nostalgia* receiving any award. (I.C.)
2 The screenplay contains the motif of flight by Alexander, but this did not appear in the finished film.
3 *Letters from a Dead Man* (1986), a post-nuclear apocalyptic fable, was directed by Konstantin Lopushansky, who had worked as a student assistant on the production of *Stalker*.

Epilogue

1 'I strove long . . .' by Arseniy Tarkovsky.

Biographical note

Andrey Arsenevich Tarkovsky was born on 4 April 1932 in Zavrozhie, near Yurievo on the Volga, to Maria Vishnyakova and Arseniy Tarkovsky. In 1939, he began school in Moscow, but was evacuated back to the Volga after the German invasion in 1941. The family returned to Moscow in 1943; and in 1945 he entered a school which specialized in art (where one of his contemporaries was the poet Andrey Voznesensky). He enrolled at the Oriental Institute in 1951 but left two years later to join a Far East expedition. He successfully applied to enter the Institute of Cinematography, VGIK, in 1954 and joined the directors' course supervised by Mikhail Romm, graduating in 1960. Later he taught at the Higher Courses in Film Direction in Moscow. The discovery of a 1964 radio play by Tarkovsky, based on William Faulkner's *Turnabout*, has recently been reported by Hans-Joachim Schlegel.

Tarkovsky visited Italy in 1980 to prepare a project which eventually became *Nostalgia*. On 10 July 1984, he announced in Milan that he would not return to the USSR since he had received inadequate assurances about his professional and personal future. Thereafter, he lived in Italy, Germany and Paris. He died in Paris on 29 December 1986, leaving a widow, Larisa, who had worked with him on all his films since *Mirror*. His first wife, Irma Raush, had appeared as an actress in *Ivan's Childhood* and *Andrey Rublyov*.

A collection of writings, prepared in collaboration with Olga Surkova, was published in Germany as *Die versiegelte Zeit* and in Britain as *Sculpting in Time* in 1986. On 4 April 1987, the Soviet cinema profession paid tribute to Tarkovsky with a special screening of *The Sacrifice* in Moscow, preceded by the first Soviet screening of *Nostalgia*. In 1988, the existence of a longer version of *Andrey Rublyov* was first revealed. An International Tarkovsky Symposium in Moscow in April 1989 led to the formation of a Tarkovsky Society and the first award of a Tarkovsky Prize, which went to the animator Yuri Norstein. Norstein announced that part of the prize will contribute to the conversion of the house on Shipok Street, where Tarkovsky lived, into a memorial museum. As this book went to press in 1989, the death of Arseniy Tarkovsky was announced.

Filmography

Credit abbreviations used follow the conventions of the British Film Institute's *Monthly Film Bulletin*, which has also provided the basis of the credits compiled here. The abbreviations are: *p.c* – Production Company; *p* – Producer; *p. sup* – Production Supervisor; *P. manager* – Production Manager; *asst. d* – Assistant Director; *sc* – Script; *ph* – Photography; *camera op* – Camera Operator; *ed* – Editor; *a.d* Art Director; *sp. effects* – Special Effects; *m* – Music; *m. d* – Music Director; *cost* – costumes; *sd* – Sound; *l.p* – Leading Players.

A. Films directed by Tarkovsky

There Will Be No Leave Today (*Segodnya uvolneniya ne budet*)
Short film made during studies at VGIK, 1959.

The Steamroller and the Violin (*Katok i stripka*)
p.c – Mosfilm. *p. sup* – A. Karetin. *asst. d* – O. Gerts. *sc* – Andrey Mikhalkov-Konchalovsky, Andrey Tarkovsky. *ph* – Vadim Yusov. Sovcolour. *ed* – L. Butuzova. *a.d* – S. Agoyan. *sp. effects* – B. Pluynikov, V. Sevostyanov, A. Rudashenko. *m* – Vyacheslav Ovchinnikov. *m.d* – E. Khachachurian. *cost* – A. Martinson. *sd* – V. Krashkovsky.

l.p – Igor Fomshenko (*Sasha*), V. Samansky (*Sergei*), Nina Arkhanelskaya (*Girl*), Marina Adzhubey (*Mother*), Yura Brusev, Slava Borisov, Sasha Vitoslavsky, Sasha Ilin, Kolya Kozarev, Gena Klyashkovsky, Igor Kolovikov, Tanya Prokhorova, A. Maksimova, L. Semyonova, M. Figner.

Made to fulfil VGIK Diploma requirement in 1960. *Length*: 46 mins.

Ivan's Childhood (*Ivanovo destvo*)
p.c – Mosfilm. *f.sup* – G. Kuznetsov. *sc* – Mikhail Papava and Vladimir Bogomolov. Based on the latter's novella, *Ivan*. *addit. sc* – E. Smirnov. *ph* – Vadim Yusov. B/W. *ed* – G. Natanson. *a.d* – Evgeni Cherniaev. *sp. effects* – V. Sevostyanov, S. Mukhin.

TARKOVSKY

m – Vyacheslav Ovchinnikov. *m.d* – E. Khachachurian. *sd* – E. Zelentsova. *military adviser* – G. Goncharov.

l.p – Kolya Burlyaev (*Ivan*), Valentin Zubkov (*Captain Kholin*), E. Zharikov (*Lieutenant Galtsev*), S. Krylov (*Corporal Katasonych*), Nikolai Grinko (*Lt-Col. Gryaznov*), L. Malyavina *(Masha)*, Irma Tarkovskaya (*Ivan's mother*), D. Milyutenko (*Old Man*), Andrey Mikhalkov-Konchalovsky (*Soldier with glasses*), Ivan Savkin, V. Marenkov, Vera Miturich.

Production: 1961–2. *Release*: 1962. *Length*: 95 mins.

Andrey Rublyov
p.c – Mosfilm. *sc* – Andrey Mikhalkov-Konchalovsky, Andrey Tarkovsky. *ph* – Vadim Yusov. Scope, B/W and part Sovcolour. *ed* – Ludmila Feganova. *a.d* – Evgeni Cherniaev. *m* – Vyacheslav Ovchinnikov. *sd* – E. Zelentsova.

l.p – Anatoly Solonitsyn (*Andrey Rublyov*), Ivan Lapikov (*Kirill*), Nikolai Grinko (*Daniel the Black*), Nikolai Sergeyev (*Theophanes the Greek*), Irma Raush Tarkovskaya (*Deaf-mute girl*), Nikolai [Kolya] Burlyaev (*Boriska*), Rolan Bykov (*Buffoon*), Yuri Nikulin (*Patrikey*), Mikhail Kononov (*Fomka*), Yuri Nazarov (*Grand Duke/his brother*), S. Krylov (*Bell-founder*), Bolot Ishalenev (*Tatar Khan*), Sos Sarkissyan, N. Grabbe, B. Matisik, Volodya Titov.

Original scenario title: The Passion According to Andrey. *Production*: 1964–6. *First screening*: 1966. *USSR release*: 1971. *UK release*: 1973. *Original length*: 185 mins. *Other release versions*: 146 mins. [*Note*: An 'ur version' of *Rublyov*, running reportedly some 60 mins longer than the previous longest known, was first shown in Moscow in April 1988, during the Dom Kino commemoration of Tarkovsky's death.]

Solaris
p.c – Mosfilm. *sc* – Andrey Tarkovsky, Friedrich Gorenstein. Based on the novel by Stanislaw Lem. *ph* – Vadim Yusov. Scope, Sovcolour. *ed* – Ludmila Feganova. *a.d* – Mikhail Romadin. *m* – Eduard Artemiev and J. S. Bach (Choral Prelude in F minor).

l.p – Natalia Bondarchuk (*Hari*), Donatas Banionis (*Chris Kelvin*), Yuri Jarvet (*Snaut*), Anatoly Solonitsyn (*Sartorius*), Vladislav Dvorzhetsky (*Burton*), Nikolai Grinko (*Kelvin's father*), Sos Sarkissyan (*Gibaryan*).

Production: 1969–72. *Release*: 1972. *Length*: 165 mins (some release versions 144 mins).

Mirror (Zerkalo)
p.c – Mosfilm, Unit 4. *p* – E. Vaisberg. *p. manager* – Y. Kushnerov. *asst. d* – Larisa Tarkovskaya, V. Karchenko, M. Chugunova. *sc* – Andrey Tarkovsky, Aleksandr

Misharin. *ph* – Georgy Rerberg. Sovcolour (newsreel sequences B/W). *camera op* – A. Nikolaev, I. Shtanko. *lighting* – V. Gusev. *ed* – Ludmila Feganova. *a.d.* – Nikolai Dvigubsky. *sets* – A. Merkunov. *sp. effects* – Y. Potapov. *m* – Eduard Artemiev, J. S. Bach, Giovanni Batista Pergolesi, Henry Purcell. *cost* – N. Fomina. *make-up* – V. Rudina. *sd* – Semyon Litvinov. *poems* – Arseniy Tarkovsky, read by the poet.

l.p – Margarita Terekhova (*Aleksei's mother/Natalia*), Filipp Yankovsky (*Ignat, aged five*), Ignat Daniltsev (*Aleksei/Ignat, aged twelve*), Oleg Yankovsky (*Father*), Nikolai Grinko (*Man at Printing Shop*), Alla Demidova (*Lisa*), Yuri Nazarov (*Military Instructor*), Anatoly Solonitsyn (*Passer-by*), Innokenti Smoktunovsky (*Voice of Aleksei, the Narrator*), Larisa Tarkovskaya (*Aleksei's mother as an older woman*), Tamara Ogorodnikova, Y. Sventikov, T. Reshetnikova, E. del Bosque, L. Correcher, A. Gutierres, D. Garcia, T. Pames, Teresa del Bosque, Tamara del Bosque.

Production: 1973–4. *USSR release*: 1974. *UK release*: 1980. *Length*: 106 mins.

Stalker
p.c – Mosfilm, Unit 2. *p. group* – T. Aleksandrovskaya, V. Vdovina, M. Mosenkov. *p. sup* – Aleksandra Demidova. *p. manager* – Larisa Tarkovskaya. *asst. d* – M. Chugunova, Evgeny Tsimbal. *sc* – Arkady and Boris Strugatsky. Based on their story, 'Roadside Picnic'. *ph* – Aleksandr Knyazhinsky. Colour. *camera op* – N. Fudim, S. Naugolnikh. *asst. camera op* – G. Verkhovsky, S. Zaitsev. *lighting sup* – L. Kazmin. *asst. lighting* – T. Maslennikova. *ed* – Ludmila Feganova. *asst. ed* – T. Alekseyeva, V. Lobkova. *p. designer* – Andrey Tarkovsky. *sets* – A. Merkulov. *artists* – R. Safiullin, V. Fabrikov. *m* – Eduard Artemiev. *m.d* – E. Khachachurian. *m. sup* – R. Lukina. *cost* – N. Fomina. *make-up* – V. Lvova. *sd* – V. Sharun.

l.p – Aleksandr Kaidanovsky (*The Stalker*), Anatoly Solonitsyn (*The Writer*), Nikolai Grinko (*The Professor/Scientist*), Alisa Freindlikh (*The Stalker's wife*), Natasha Abramova, F. Yurna, E. Kostin, R. Rendi.

Original scenario title: The Wish Machine. *First screening*: 1979. *Length*: 161 mins.

Nostalgia (Nostalghia)
p.c – Opera Film (Rome), for RAI TV Rete 2; in association with Sovinfilm (USSR). *exec. p* – Renzo Rossellini, Manolo Bolognini. *p* – Francesco Casati. *p. exec* – Lorenzo Ostuni (RAI). *p. sup* – Filippo Campus, Valentino Signoretti. *p. admin* – Nestore Baratella. *asst. d* – Norman Mozzato, Larisa Tarkovsky. *sc* – Andrey Tarkovsky, Tonino Guerra. *ph* – Giuseppe Lanci. Eastman Color. *camera op* – Giuseppe De Biasi. *ed* – Erminia Marani, Amedeo Salfa. *asst. ed* – Roberto Puglisi. *a.d* – Andrea Crisanti. *set dresser* – Mauro Passi. *m* – (not credited). *m. consultant* – Gino Peguri. *cost* – Lina Nerli Taviani, Annamode 68. *make-up sup* – Giulio Mastrantonio. *sd. rec* – Remo Ugolinelli. *sd. mixer* – Danilo Moroni. *sd. re-rec* – Filippo Ottoni, Ivana Fidele. *sd. effects* – Massimo Anzellotti, Luciano Anzellotti.

l.p – Oleg Yankovsky (*Andrey Gorchakov*), Erland Josephson (*Domenico*), Domiziana Giordano (*Eugenia*), Patrizia Terreno (*Gorchakov's wife*), Laura De Marchi (*Woman with towel*), Delia Boccardo (*Domenico's wife*), Milena Vukotic (*Town worker*), Alberto Canepa (*Peasant*), Raffaele Di Mario, Rate Furlan, Livio Galassi, Piero Vida, Elena Magoia.

Production: 1981–3. *Release*: 1983. *Length*: 126 mins.

The Sacrifice (*Offret*)
p.c – Swedish Film Institute (Stockholm)/Argos Film (Paris). In association with Film Four International. Josephson & Nykvist, Sveriges Television/SVT 2, Sandrew Film & Teater. With the participation of the French Ministry of Culture. *exec. p* – Anna-Lena Wibom (Swedish Film Institute). *p* – Katinka Farago (Farago Film). *p. man* – Goran Lindberg. *casting* – Priscilla John, Claire Denis, Françoise Menidrey. *asst. d* – Kerstin Eriksdotter, (post-p.) Michal Leszczylowski. *sc* – Andrey Tarkovsky. *ph* – Sven Nykvist. Eastman Colour, B/W. *camera op* – Lasse Karlsson, Dan Myhrman. *ed* – Andrey Tarkovsky, Michal Leszczylowski. *ed. consultant* – Henri Colpi. *a.d* – Anna Asp. *sp. effects* – Svenska Stuntgruppen; Lars Hoglund, Lara Palmqvist. *m* – J. S. Bach, *St Matthew Passion*; Swedish and Japanese folk music. *cost* – Inger Pehrsson. *make-up* – Kjell Gustavsson, Florence Fouquier. *sd. rec/re-rec* – Owe Svenson, Bosse Persson, Lars Ulander, Christin Lohman, Wikee Peterson-Berger. *interpreter* – Layla Alexander. *technical manager* – Kaj Larsen.

l.p – Erland Josephson (*Alexander*), Susan Fleetwood (*Adelaide*), Valerie Mairesse (*Julia*), Allan Edwall (*Otto*), Gudrún Gísladóttir (*Maria*), Sven Wollter (*Victor*), Filippa Franzén (*Marta*), Tommy Kjellqvist (*Little Man*), Per Kallman, Tommy Nordahl (*Ambulancemen*).

Release: 1986. *Length*: 149 mins.

B. Other films reputedly co-scripted by Tarkovsky

The First Teacher (*Pervy uchitel*)
p.c – Kirghizfilm, Mosfilm. *d* – Andrey Mikhalkov-Konchalovsky. *Co-sc* – (uncr.) with Chingiz Aitmatov, Andrey Mikhalkov-Konchalovsky. *Release*: 1965.

Tashkent the Bread City (*Tashkent – gorod khlebnii*)
d – Shukhrat Abbasov. *co-sc* – (uncr.) with Andrey Mikhalkov-Konchalovsky. *p.c* – Uzbekfilm. *Release*: 1968.

One Chance in a Thousand (*Odin shans iz tisyachi*)
co-sc/d – L. Kosharjan. *Release*: 1969.

The End of the Chieftain (Konets atamana)
p.c – Kazakfilm. *d* – Shaken Aimanov (1914–70). *Release*: 1971.

The Ferocious One (Liuti)
d – Tolomush Okeev. *Release*: 1973.

C. Film projects announced by or attributed to Tarkovsky

A Light Breeze (Svetly veter): unpublished screenplay by Tarkovsky and Friedrich Gorenstein, based on *Ariel* by Aleksandr Belyaev.

The Idiot (Dostoevsky)

The Master and Margarita (Bulgakov)

Hoffmanniana: scenario on the life and themes of the German writer and musician E. T. A. Hoffmann, published in *Iskusstvo kino*, no. 8, 1976.

Hamlet (Shakespeare)

Select Bibliography

Writings and interviews by Andrey Tarkovsky

'Questions of Cinema Art', *Iskusstvo kino* 4, 1967.

'L'artiste dans l'ancienne russie et dans l'urss nouvelle', interview by Michel Ciment, Luda and Jean Schnitzer, *Positif* 109, 1969, pp. 1–13.

'Why was the last meeting with the future?', *Iskusstvo kino* 11, 1971, pp. 96–101.

Interview about plans for *Stalker*, *Iskusstvo kino* 3, 7, 1977, pp. 116–18.

'Andrei Tarkovsky' interview by Jacques Fieschi and Dominique Maillet, *Cinematographe* 35, 1978, pp. 25–7.

'About the Film image', *Iskusstvo kino* 3, 1979, pp. 80–93.

'Stalker' le contrabandier du bonheur', interview by Tonino Guerra, *Telerama* 1535, 13 June 1979, pp. 85–7.

'The Confessions of Andrei Tarkovsky', interview by Nick Anning, Chris Auty, *Time Out*, 6–12 March 1981, p. 10.

'Against Interpretation', interview by Ian Christie, *Framework* 14, 1981, pp. 48–9.

'Tarkovsky in Italy', interview by Tony Mitchell, *Sight and Sound*, Winter 1982–3, pp. 54–6.

'Telluride Gold: Brakhage meets Tarkovsky', interview by Stan Brakhage, *Rolling Stock* 6, 1983, pp. 11–14.

'Red Tape', interview by Angus MacKinnon, *Time Out*, 9–15 August 1984, pp. 20–2.

'Bomb Culture', interview by Angus MacKinnon, *Time Out*, 31 December 1986–7 January 1987, pp. 22–2.

Sculpting in Time (1986), in collaboration with Olga Surkova, includes extracts and reworkings of earlier articles, together with new material. A second revised edition published by Faber and Faber in 1989.

Martyrolog: Tagebücher 1970–86, Berlin, Limes, 1989.

Critical writings about Tarkovsky

'Man and Experience: Tarkovsky's World', Ivor Montagu, *Sight and Sound*, Spring 1973, pp. 89–94.

'Andrei Tarkovsky's *The Mirror*', Herbert Marshall, *Sight and Sound*, Spring 1976, pp. 92–5.

'Solaris', Timothy Hyman, *Film Quarterly*, March 1976.

Positif 247, 1981: special dossier on Tarkovsky.

Andreï Tarkovsky, edited by Michel Estève, Études Cinématographiques nos. 135–8, Paris 1983; includes articles by Jean-Paul Sartre, Barthélemy Amengual, Michel Ciment, Michel Estève, France Farago, Jacques Gerstenkorn, Marcel Martin, Gerard Pangon, François Ramasse, Sylvie Strudel and Marie-Claude Tigoulet.

A.T.: Film als Poesie, Poesie als Film, Maya Turovskaya, Bonn, 1981.

'La maison où il pleut: sur l'esthetique de Tarkovski', Michel Chion, *Cahiers du cinéma* 358, April 1984, pp. 37–43.

'The Nostalgia of the Stalker', Peter Green, *Sight and Sound*, Winter 1984–5, pp. 50–4.

The Films of Andrei Tarkovsky, catalogue of retrospective at the Hopkins Center of Dartmouth College, Hanover, New Hampshire, 1986; with programme notes by Barry Scherr and an introduction by Ian Christie.

'Raising the Shroud', Ian Christie, *Monthly Film Bulletin*, February 1987, pp. 37–8.

The Cinema of Andrei Tarkovsky, Mark Le Fanu, London, 1987.

'Eisenstein et Tarkovski: au-delà des images', François Albera, *Rectangle* 20/21, March–April 1988, pp. 32–3.

Index

Abalov, E., 29–30
Alov, Aleksandr, 20
Alphaville, 52
Amarcord, 65, 105
Andrey Rublyov, xiv, xx, 20, 22, 23, 36–50, 75, 108; actors, 45, 83, 125–6; battle scene, 41–3, 47, 90–1, 139; childhood motif, 89; church setting, 80; delay in being released, x, 49, 152–3; editing, 47–8; epilogue, 46, 54, 79, 81; episodic structure, 37–44, 86; 'flying peasant' prologue, xix, 36, 47–8, 77–8; motif of the Trinity, 38, 54, 113; rain motif, 81; reception, 48–9, 52, 136; in retrospect, 152–3; screenplay, 47; setting, 33, 88, 90, 151; stuttering, 80–1; success, 136–7; time in, xxi–xxii, 87; violence, 39–40, 41–3, 95
Andropov, Yuri, xi
April, xiii
L'Argent, 136
art, xxii, 67, 91–2, 139
Artemiev, Eduard, 110, 144
Asya's Happiness, 151
Auden, W. H., xix
Auschwitz museum, 47
'*auteur*' cinema, 33
Autumn Violins, 143

Bach, J. S., 67, 91, 92, 138, 149
Bagno, Vignoni, 121–2

Balazs, Bela, 95
The Ballad of a Soldier, 31, 34
Battleship Potemkin, xviii
Bazin, André, xx, 85
Beethoven, Ludwig van, 92, 128, 133
Bergman, Ingmar, 20, 33, 75, 130, 137
Blok, Aleksandr, 3, 43–4, 56
Bogomolov, Vladimir, 2, 4, 30–2, 33, 76, 83, 96, 97
Borges, Jorge Luis, xxv
Boule de Suif, 21
Bresson, Robert, xxiii, 20, 33, 75, 136
Brezhnev, Leonid, xi, xiii
Bright, Bright Day, 62–3
Brodsky, Joseph, 85
Brown, Clarence, xxv–xxvi
Brueghel, Pieter, 56, 67, 89–90, 92
Buñuel, Luis, 20, 33
Burlyaev, Kolya, 30, 44–5, 125

Can This Be Love?, xviii
Cannes Film Festival, 18, 48, 57, 94–5, 97, 136
Chaliapin, Fyodor, 7, 9, 97
Chapayev, 25
Chekhov, Anton, 17, 137, 143, 152
Chernenko, Konstantin, xi
Chernobyl, 115–16
Cherniaev, Evgení, 29
childhood motif, 82–3, 84; in *Andrey Rublyov*, 89; in *Ivan's Childhood*, 32, 35; in *Mirror*, 65, 105; in *The*

INDEX

Sacrifice, 138; in *Stalker*, 114, 115; in *The Steamroller and the Violin*, 22–7
Christian symbolism, 79–80, 113, 128
Chudakov, Seriozha, 45
Chukhrai, Grigory, 27, 31
church motif, 79–80, 113
Cinema Institute, 16, 17
The Clear Sky, 31
colour, in *Stalker*, 110
The Concentrate, 19–20
Confession, 61–2
The Cranes Are Flying, 18, 34

Danela, Georgy, xiii
documentary film, newsreels, 62, 67, 79, 86–7, 90, 91, 128
La Dolce Vita, 37, 75, 115, 127
Dom Kino, xxv, 150
Dostoevsky, Fyodor, xxii, 58, 63, 108, 139–40
The Dream, 21
dreams, 50, 87–8; in *Ivan's Childhood*, 31–2, 76–7; in *Nostalgia*, 128–30; in *The Sacrifice*, 145–8; in *Stalker*, 114
Dürer, Albrecht, xvii, 4, 5, 91

Edval, Allan, 139
Efros, 11
8½, 75, 105
Eisenstein, Sergei, xii–xiii, xvii–xviii, xix–xxx, 37, 43
The Exterminator, xiv

family relationships, 84, 114, 138
fatherhood, 83, 84, 138
Favorsky, Vladimir, 11
Fellini, Federico, xvii, 20, 33, 65, 75, 105, 115, 127
film festivals, 34, 57
Film-Makers' Union, x, xi, xiii, xxiv, 1, 34, 95, 150
fire motif, 82, 132–3, 148–9
The First Teacher, xiv, 20–1
Five Year Plans, 45
flash-backs, 87
Fleetwood, Susan, 142–3

flight motif, 77–9, 82, 92, 114, 147
Ford, John, xvii
Formalists, 101
The Forty-First, 31
Frantzén, Filippa, 143
Freindlikh, Alisa, 114

Gísladóttir, Gudrún, 144
Glickenhaus, James, xiv
Godard, Jean-Luc, 52
Goebbels, Joseph, 5, 8
Gogol, Nikolai, 120
Goskino, ix, x, xxiv, xxv, 117
Grinko, Nikolai, 83–4, 112, 125
Guerra, Tonino, 118, 120, 121, 122, 126

Hamlet, 126
Heat, xiii
Hitchcock, Alfred, 52
Hitler, Adolf, 67, 90
'Holy fools', 109
home motif, 141–2
horror films, 56
The House Where I Live, 18

I Am Twenty, xiii
The Idiot, xxii, 108
Ioseliani, Otar, xi, xiii
Italy, 117, 119–24, 137
Ivan the Terrible, xix–xxx, 37
Ivanov, Vyacheslav, 92–3
Ivanovo district, 15
Ivan's Childhood, x, xiii, xvii, xviii, xxi, 1–11, 29–35, 43, 47, 75, 95, 108; actors, 30; art in, 91; childhood motif, 32, 35; church motif, 79–80, 113; death of the mother, 3, 83; dream sequences, 31–2, 76–7; epilogue, 8, 9–10, 100; filming, 33–4; imagery, 8–9; 'Lyakhov and Morozov' theme, 8, 96–7; plot, 1–8, 31; prologue, 2, 54, 79; rain motif, 81; in retrospect, 152; structure, 97; stuttering, 80; time in, xxi–xxii, 92;

174

INDEX

use of newsreels, 4–5, 87; at Venice Film Festival, 34, 48

Josephson, Erland, 109, 125, 127, 130, 141, 146

Kaidanovsky, Aleksandr, xxv, 108, 112
Kalatozov, Mikhail, 18
Kanev, 33
Khrushchev, Nikita, xii, xiii, xiv
Khutsiev, Marlen, xiii, 27
Kino nedelya, xxiv
Klimov, Elem, xiii–xxiv
Komsomolskaya Pravda, 31
Kracauer, Siegfried, 43
Kramer vs Kramer, xv
Kubrick, Stanley, 52, 57, 59
Kulidzhanov, Lev, 18
Kulikovo Polye, 47, 48, 90
Kureika, river, 16–17
Kurosawa, Akira, 20, 81

Lanchi, 122
Lem, Stanislaw, 51–3, 55, 59, 76
Lenfilm Studios, xxv
Lenin, xii, xv, 21
Lenin in 1918, 21
Lenin in October, 21
Lenin Komsomol Theatre, 126
Leningrad, xxv
Leonardo da Vinci, 42, 67, 91, 138–9, 145, 146, 147, 148
Letters from a Dead Man, xxv, 146
Literary Gazette, 1
Literary Institute, Moscow, 15
Lopushansky, Konstantin, xxv
love themes, 66, 122–3

Madonna, 120, 124, 139
Mairesse, Valerie, 144
Mandelstam, Osip, xxv–xxvi, 75
Mao Tse-tung, 90
memory, 68, 87–8
metaphor, Tarkovsky's dislike of, 19, 78
Michelangelo, xxi

Mikhalkov-Konchalovsky, Andrey, xi, xiv, 20–1, 22, 36–7, 151
minimalism: in *Stalker*, 107, 109–10, 114, 120; in *A Time to Travel*, 120
Mirror, 37, 61–9, 75; actors, 82, 83–4, 125, 126; art in, 42, 67, 91, 139; childhood in, 65, 105; church motif, 80; documentary elements, 66; editing, 69, 71; fire motif, 82; first versions, 61–4; flight motif, 78–9; Kulikovo battle scene, 47, 90–1; motherhood motif, 68–9, 84; prologue, 64; rain motif, 81; in retrospect, 153–4; settings, 15, 16, 89–90, 142; structure, 99; stuttering, 64, 80–1; time in, xxi–xxii, 67, 87, 91, 92; use of newsreels, 67, 87
mirrors, 26, 81
Mizoguchi, Kenzo, xvii
Mon Oncle d'Amérique, xiv
Moscow Arts Theatre, 143
Moscow Elegy, xxv
Mosfilm Studios, x, xii, 22, 29, 32, 69; Children's and Youth Films section, 26; Second Production Group, 106
motherhood, 68–9, 83, 84
motifs, 75–84
music, 91, 92, 97, 110, 124

narrative structure, 94, 97
naturalism, 50
nature motifs, 81–2, 114
Naumov, Vladimir, 20
neo-realism, 18, 33
newsreels, 62, 67, 79, 86–7, 90, 91, 128
Nietzsche, Friedrich Wilhelm, 140
Nine Days of One Year, xii, 21
Nostalgia, xix, 117, 118–35; actors, 125–6; at Cannes Film Festival, 136; central character, 120–1, 126–7; coda, 132–4; dream sequence, 128–30; motifs, 124–5; plot, 118–19; in retrospect, 153; settings, 119–23, 127–8; time in, xxi, 131

175

INDEX

nouvelle vague, xii
Nykvist, Sven, 137

Oberhausen Film Festival, 45
October, xviii
Ogorodnikova, Tamara, 83
An Ordinary Death, xxv
Ordinary Fascism, 21
Ordzhonikidze, Sergo, 45
Oriental Institute, 16
Ostrovsky, Aleksandr, 79

Panofsky, Erwin, xvi–xvii
Papava, M., 31
Paradzhanov, Sergey, xi, xiv
Pasolini, Pier Paolo, 63
The Passion According to Andrey, 108
Pasternak, Boris, 57, 62, 94, 100
Pavlov, Ivan Petrovich, 100
Piero della Francesca, 121, 124, 139, 147
Plato, xv
poetry, cinema as, 94–101
Proust, Marcel, 82, 105
Purcell, Henry, 67, 79, 91
Pushkin, Aleksandr, xxvi, 80, 90

rain motif, 81–2, 124, 128
Raizman, Yuli, x, xviii
religious symbolism, 79–80, 113
Renaissance, 67, 124
Renoir, Jean, xii
Rerberg, Georgy, 65
Resnais, Alain, xiv
rhythm, 99–100
A Roadside Picnic, 106
Romm, Mikhail, xi–xiii, xvii, xxiii, 1, 17–18, 20, 21
Rousseau, Jean-Jacques, 62
Rozov, Viktor, 18
Rublyov, Andrey, 36–8; *see also Andrey Rublyov*
Ruza, river, 53

The Sacrifice, 125, 136–50; dream sequence, 145–8, epilogue, 148–9;
importance of spoken word, 139–40; motifs, 138; in retrospect, 155; setting, 137, 138–9, 141–3; soundtrack, 144; time in, xxi
St James's Church, London, xxv
Salt for Svanetia, 18
Savvino-Storozhevsky Monastery, 53
science fiction, 51-60, 93, 95, 106–7, 110, 111–12, 143, 152
Sculpting in Time, xix, xx, 118
Second World War, 2–9, 31–2
Segel, Yakov, 18
Seryozha, xiii
settings, 88–90
Seurat, Georges, xvii
Shadows of Our Forgotten Ancestors, xiv
Shakespeare, William, xvii, 139–40
Shepitko, Larissa, xiii
Shklovsky, Victor, 10, 101
Sholokhov, Mikhail, 3
Shukshin, Vasily, xiii, xiv
Siberia, 115
Sinyavsky, Andrey, xiii
Skanderbeg, xvii, 18–19
Skriabin, Aleksandr, xxv–xxvi
Socrates, xv, 92
Sokurov, Aleksandr, xxv
Solaris, 51–60, 106; actors, 64, 83; art in, 91–2; audience reactions to, 57–8, 94–5; church motif, 80; Hari's shawl, 97–8; plot, 51–2, 53, 56–7; prologue, 53–4, 76; in retrospect, 152; settings, 53–4, 82, 89, 90; soundtrack, 110, 144; success, 136–7; time in, 92; weightlessness, 78–9
Solo, xxv
Solonitsyn, Anatoly, 64–5, 112, 125–6, 130, 133, 140
sound, 144
space, 92–3
Spanish Civil War, 67
Stalin, Joseph, xi, xii, xv, xxvi, 67
Stalker, ix, 106–16, 117, 118; actors, xxv, 112; central character, 108–9, 112, 126–7; childhood in, 114, 115; filming, x, 110–11; minimalism, 107,

176

109–10, 114, 120; motifs, 113–14; in retrospect, 154; screenplay, 106–9; setting, xix, 111–12, 142; soundtrack, 110, 144; success, 136–7
Stanislavsky, Konstantin, 80
State Committee for the Cinema, 48
The Steamroller and the Violin, xiv, xviii, 20, 22–8, 75, 81, 84, 94, 99, 151
The Storm, 79
Strugatsky brothers, 106–7, 110
stuttering motif, 80–1
Surguchev, 143
Surin, 29
Sweden, 136, 137
Swedish Film Institute, 136

Tarkovsky, Andrey: childhood, 15–16, 17; expedition to Turukhansky region, 16–17; at VGIK, 17–21; influence of Buñuel and Bergman, 20; Romm's influence, 21; collaboration with Mikhalkov-Konchalovsky, 20–1, 22; professionalism, 33–4; motifs, 75–84; choice of actors, 83–4; chronotype, 85–93; in the West, 117–18, 136; ill-health, 137, 145, 153–4; Memorial Retrospective, 150; *see also individual films*
Tarkovsky, Arseniy Aleksandrovich, 15–16, 22, 66, 68, 69, 90, 123, 129–30, 133, 150, 152, 154
television, 61–2, 153
Terekhova, Margarita, 66, 139
Theophanes, 40
There Was a Lad, xiv
time, xx–xxii, 67, 68–9, 85–8, 90–2, 131, 152
A Time to Travel, 120–2
Tolstoy, Leo, xxv
Tretyakov, Sergey, 18

Trinity motif, 38, 54, 79, 80, 113, 141
Turukhansky region, 16–17
Twentieth Party Congress, xii, 27
Two Fyodors, xiii
2001: A Space Odyssey, 52, 57
Tyutchev, Fedor, 114–15, 143

Union of Cinematographers, 69
Urusevsky, Sergey, 3, 18

Venice Film Festival, 34, 48, 152
VGIK, xi, xii, xiii, xix, 17–21
'VGIK school', 17–18
Vietnam war, 62
Vigo, Jean, 33
violence, 4–5, 58
Vishnyakova, Maria Ivanovna (Tarkovsky's mother), 15–16, 61–2, 69
Volga, river, 15, 16
Voznesensky, Andrey, 36, 37, 43, 44

Welcome, or No Unauthorised Entry, xiv
'Weldschmertz', 125
When the Leaves Fall, xiii
Wibom, Anna-Lena, 136
'wife–mother' duality, 63–4, 124
Wild Strawberries, 75
The Wish Machine, 106–7
Wollter, Sven, 143

Yankovsky, Oleg, 125, 126–7, 130, 133
Yermash, Filip, x
Yurievo, 15
Yusov, Vadim, 25, 29
Yutkevich, Sergey, xvii–xviii, 18

Zavrozhie, 15
Zen Buddhism, xxii
Zvenigorod, 53